The Girl for
the Job

Danni Brooke

The Girl for the Job

True stories from my life as an undercover cop

MACMILLAN

First published 2023 by Macmillan
an imprint of Pan Macmillan
The Smithson, 6 Briset Street, London EC1M 5NR
EU representative: Macmillan Publishers Ireland Ltd, 1st Floor,
The Liffey Trust Centre, 117–126 Sheriff Street Upper,
Dublin 1, D01 YC43
Associated companies throughout the world
www.panmacmillan.com

ISBN 978-1-0350-0669-4

1 3 5 7 9 8 6 4 2

A CIP catalogue record for this book is available from the British Library.

Typeset in Stempel Garamond LT Pro by Palimpsest Book Production Limited,
Falkirk, Stirlingshire
Printed and bound by CPI Group (UK) Ltd, Croydon, CR0 4YY

Visit **www.panmacmillan.com** to read more about all our books
and to buy them. You will also find features, author interviews and
news of any author events, and you can sign up for e-newsletters
so that you're always first to hear about our new releases.

To my Amelia, Albert & Ben –
and my parents, all four of them

Contents

DISCLAIMER: Everything that you read in this book happened to me, but I have changed names, dates and places to protect the identity and privacy of certain individuals.

Prologue

What am I doing? What the hell am I doing?

I stamped my numb feet against the cold, hard pavement and shivered. It was a freezing day in February and I was dressed in the tiniest chequered blue skirt, a thin jumper, knee-high socks and a blazer. A school uniform! I was almost thirty years old, for god's sake, and a mum! Casually, I slung the rucksack with the surveillance camera over my shoulder and sauntered up the road, as if waiting for a friend to arrive. Two weeks I'd been on this job. Two weeks of standing on street corners in the biting wind of a winter's morning without any results. I glanced up at the litter pickers moving up and down the street, the bin men shuttling in and out of driveways and the suited man slumped at the bus stop – all part of our surveillance team. All of us freezing cold.

The operation was being run by an older female detective inspector who was coming up on retirement. DI Philips liked to moan about the early mornings from the comparative warmth of her car, then had the cheek to tell me off for putting on a coat. That really wound me up. It had happened around the third day of the job. I'd spent the first two mornings gradually turning hypothermic in an effort to catch a sexual predator who had been attacking girls on their way to school for the past six months. Some of the girls had been attacked more than once, even after changing their route to school. He was a pretty sick individual, this guy – chasing young girls, lifting their skirts, trying to touch them before running away. He was now wanted for over a hundred offences on girls as young as twelve. There seemed to be no obvious links between the victims other than the fact that they were all young and, with one exception, schoolgirls. He wasn't choosey, this predator – he had attacked girls of all different ages, builds, ethnicities and clothing. Naturally, the community was worried and the police were doing everything they could to catch him. But he wasn't daft, managing to avoid any areas covered by CCTV. Right now, all we had to go on was an e-fit from witness statements. I'd been tasked with standing around in the leafy suburbs of north London, dressed up like an unsuspecting schoolgirl for two hours each morning in the hope of luring him out for the camera. But after my morning shift undercover, I couldn't get warm for the rest of the day. I was frozen to my bones. So, on the third morning, I'd added a navy parka to the ensemble.

'What's that?' the DI had stopped me as I was on my way out.

'It's a coat,' I'd said, straight-faced.

'Well, take it off. You can't see the school skirt underneath.'

Fucking hell, I'd thought as I eased my arms out of the warm, fleece-lined coat. *He's not coming for me, coat or no coat!* It was a well-known fact that decoy jobs weren't usually successful. In all my time working as an undercover officer I'd only ever heard of two that had worked. For the most part, they were a last throw of the dice, a way of showing senior management that we were literally trying everything to catch the suspects.

Don't get me wrong, I enjoyed decoy jobs. They could be great fun. I'd spent many memorable afternoons hanging round in parks with other undercover officers, drinking booze in the late-afternoon sunshine, trying to get mugged. For one job, there had been a spate of robberies around Greenwich in south London – a group of lads nicking laptops, phones, watches, anything they could find, really. Me and another female undercover officer (or UC) were tasked with trying to attract them. So we sat on the grass, sipping from tinnies, our smartphones blatantly on display, occasionally tapping on laptops, but no . . . not a peep. Still, I'd been paid to sit in the park on four summer's evenings. What's not to like? We'd done our best to look as vulnerable as possible, but it hadn't worked.

Another time I was sent to catch a rapist in Brixton. There had been a number of sexual assaults and one rape in the area, all within a short time period, and the descriptions from the victims matched a guy already known to the police.

'We have a pretty good idea who it is,' the UC officer leading the job told me. 'We just have to catch him at it.' So I was roped in to try and stop him in his tracks. It was late on a Friday night when I arrived at the location where we knew he had been operating. I couldn't very well just hop out of a police car and stand around waiting to be attacked – it had to look as authentic as possible. So I walked to reach the prearranged area where the rest of the surveillance team were stationed.

As I turned the corner in my short dress and towering heels, I started to stagger and lurch, pretending to be drunk. Young, female, drunk, alone – here I was, the perfect target for any would-be attacker. *Come and get me!* As luck would have it, just as I teetered past the pub where we knew the suspect had been drinking, he actually came out. This was too good to be true. I fell over and dropped my bag, emptying the contents all over the pavement. He was coming over!

This is it. This is it . . . I thought, bracing myself for the inevitable. I wasn't scared. Not at all. I knew that whatever was coming the surveillance team were close by, ready to pounce.

'There you go, love.' The guy picked up my purse and handed it to me.

'Er, thanks,' I said, confused, taking the purse.

'Go on, put it back in the bag,' he urged, collecting up my keys, lipstick and phone. 'Go on. You don't want to be losing all your stuff.'

'No, s'pose not,' I slurred weakly. *Shit, what's happening?* Instead of bundling me down a dark alley, the alleged rapist was acting like the perfect gentleman. I couldn't believe it. Neither could the rest of the team when we debriefed back at the station.

'You could have fallen on him a bit,' one suggested unhelp-fully.

'What? No I couldn't!'

'Nah, Danni wasn't his cup of tea,' joked another officer. It was dead serious, of course, but when you're working these types of jobs, a little banter helps to lighten the mood. It had been a long shot and we all knew it.

Which brings me back to the schoolgirl job. I breathed out clouds of warm air into the crisp morning. It was nearly 9.30 a.m. – well after the start of the school day. I was even more conspicuous than I'd been at 7.30 a.m., when I'd first appeared, and the chances of this guy making an appearance so late in the day were practically zero. I could no longer feel my feet, my fingers were frozen stiff and my legs had gone blotchy red from the cold. The phone in my pocket buzzed. It was DI Philips, a resigned note in her voice: 'Okay, let's wrap this up, Danni. Come back to the safety location.'

I was disappointed, of course. I'd been out every morning the past two weeks trying to catch this bastard and today was our last day. *Damn.* After all that work, I really wanted to get this guy.

I started walking back to the safety location but noticed a shadow out of the corner of my eye, someone acting odd behind me. I glimpsed a guy in a black hat, peeking round the bush of a corner house. *What is he doing?*

I carried on walking and a few seconds later, I heard foot-steps behind me. He grabbed me by my neck. The next thing I was on the floor and he was on top of me.

'Fuck!' I shouted, alarmed and confused. The safety team now sprang into action to make the arrest.

'POLICE! POLICE! POLICE!' I heard shouts all around me. 'STAY DOWN. DON'T MOVE. HANDS WHERE WE CAN SEE THEM.' My confusion gave way to the realization that we had him. The decoy plan had actually worked in the very last moments of the job. I couldn't believe it.

An officer helped me to my feet.

'Dirty twat!' I exclaimed in the vague direction of the attacker, still in shock.

'Let's get you to the safety location, Danni,' said the officer who'd helped me up. 'We'll need to get those clothes off you for evidence.'

Back at the safety location, my handler greeted me excitedly.

'We got him. We got the money shot, Danni!'

I could hardly hear him over the cheering of the rest of the team.

'We got him spunking all over your blazer. It's solid gold.'

'What?'

'Yeah, we saw it all through the camera in the rucksack. He got his dick out as he came up behind you and ejaculated all over your blazer. It's A1. Well done, you did it!'

'Dirty twat!' I said again, still in shock.

Back at the station, everyone was happy. We had just pulled off one of the most effective decoy operations the Metropolitan Police had ever carried out. The suspect was looking at a jail term and would be on the sexual offences register for life. Best of all, the streets of north London had been made safer for schoolgirls. I got a commissioner's commendation for that job – quite a rare accolade – and a few days later I received a letter of thanks from the mother of one of the repeat victims who said her daughter had been scarred for life by the attacks. Now she could sleep soundly again. It meant a lot to me, reading that letter, knowing how I'd made a real difference to someone's life.

I was pleased. We had done a good thing taking this predator off the streets. He had practically handed us the crucial evidence in his final attack, which was on me, a hardened police officer, and not on an innocent child. DI Philips was cock-a-hoop, of course. This was just the sort of win that meant she could bow out of the force on a high. Naturally, she was quick to take credit for the success of the operation. Meanwhile, I was given a week off to recuperate and see the counsellor. This was standard practice, of course, though none of us actually went to see him. It just wasn't the done thing. Undercover officers were expected to suck it up and move on to the next job. Visiting the counsellor, unburdening your troubles and trauma, could be interpreted as a sign of weakness. A stigma. Nobody wanted to be labelled 'troubled' – it could have a lasting impact on your work – so even during the obligatory psychological assessments, when I was dragged into the counsellor's office, I kept my mouth shut. *Don't talk about the stress or sleepless nights, don't moan, don't give anything away*, that was the mantra. *Say nothing, keep your head down and get on with it.* Besides, I had no complaints. I loved my job. I really did. I'd been at it for ten years by then and I was proud of the work I'd done infiltrating criminal gangs, disrupting drug supply lines and putting perverts like this guy behind bars.

So why did I wake up every day with a knot of dread in my stomach at the thought of going back to work? Why did I feel like getting as far away as possible? In the quiet moments at home, I'd look at the kids and feel an inexplicable ache. Something had changed in me, but I didn't know what it was or where eventually it would lead.

1

The Real Polly Page

I never considered joining the force until Dad suggested it. I wanted to be a hotshot lawyer, like the kind I saw on Channel 5's *LA Law*, but my dad Mark was an officer and he thought I'd enjoy police work. Him and my mum Janice divorced when I was three, and my younger brother and I grew up with Mum and our stepdad Steve in Dagenham. Unfortunately, things weren't always hunky-dory between my parents, so I didn't get to spend as much time with my dad as I would have liked until I landed a Saturday job at Sainsbury's when I was fifteen. The supermarket was near his home, so he'd come to see me at work or I'd go round to his when I clocked off. I was in the middle of five A levels and considering applying for university when Dad told me about the drive to recruit more women to the Met.

'Just go for an interview,' he suggested. 'You might not even get in but if you do, at least it gives you options.'

'Do you think I'd like it?'

'I think you'd love it, Danielle.'

I took the ad home, mulling it over. I supposed I could always send off an application and if I got in and didn't like it then I could apply to university afterwards.

'What do you want to go joining the police for? You're too little!' Mum said when I told her my plan.

I'm 5 feet 2 inches . . . 5 feet 3 inches if I stretch my neck.

'I dunno,' I shrugged. I didn't want to tell her Dad had suggested it. 'It's a good career.'

'Hmmm . . .'

Mum was a worrier and in her mind I was still her little girl, so she didn't like the idea of my joining the force. It had always been that way, and probably stemmed from the fact that I'd suffered from a critical heart condition as a child that put me under the care of Great Ormond Street Hospital. I had a hole in the heart when I was a baby, which was fairly common – but then the hole had returned when I was three years old, which was not so common. Mum had spotted an unusual rash and I was taken straight to hospital, where I was given open heart surgery. It was a difficult time, because my parents were splitting up. I made the most of the sympathy, of course, tapping up Dad for cherry Cokes and Mars bars when I was in hospital.

My baby teeth fell out all at once, a side-effect of the condition. We were told it could impact my hair, teeth and nails and I suppose I was fortunate it was just my teeth. I had no teeth at all until my adult teeth started to grow through aged ten. It made me really self-conscious. I hated having photos taken and I couldn't eat normal things like apples, which was embarrassing. Thankfully, my heart condition cleared up and my childhood was largely unaffected otherwise. The one thing that persisted was the collection tin for Great Ormond Street that sat on the front desk of

Ilford Police Station, which I think was Dad's way of trying to give something back to the people who had taken care of me as a child. Dad didn't believe my early health issues should hold me back, but I think that for Mum, I was always the small, fragile child who needed extra protection and care. I certainly didn't consider myself fragile, throwing myself into my undercover role, never believing for one moment that anything bad would happen to me. Far from it – I felt invincible.

None of Mum's family had much time for the police. The youngest of twelve, my mum came from a family of true east-enders, the kind of people who sorted their own stuff out. No one was all that thrilled when she met my dad, a copper, while he was on duty in Ilford. Even worse – she fell pregnant with me fairly soon after they started going out, which led to a shotgun wedding and a move from Mile End to Barking. But Mum's family looked out for each other and not long after our move my nan and grandad joined us in Barking so they could help out with childcare. Mum was pregnant with my brother when she and my dad split in 1986, and from then on things were fraught between them. There were plenty of times I was meant to see my dad and didn't and when he got together with my stepmum Lesley I wasn't allowed to go round their house. But I had no regrets about my parents splitting up and if you knew them, you'd know why. They were pure opposites, Mum and Dad, like chalk and cheese. It wouldn't have worked in a million years.

Mum and her family's wariness of the police wasn't just to do with my dad or a general distrust – it was practical, even sensible, considering there was so much dodgy stuff going on in her family! When I was round at Nan's she'd often have a brand-new washing machine to show off or a top-of-the-range vacuum cleaner to demonstrate – that kind of thing.

'Cor, that's nice, Nan,' I'd say admiringly. 'Where'd you get it?'

'Your uncle Stephen found it for me,' she'd reply, proudly. I remember thinking: *Well, that's nice of him.* As I got older, of course, I started to understand what it meant when things were 'found' or 'fell off the back of a lorry'. That was just how things were on my mum's side, and I learned not to ask questions if I didn't want to know the answers.

Dad was a different character altogether – sensible, quiet, law-abiding. I loved my mum and spending time with her vast, crazy family – especially my Aunty Anne and uncles Stephen and Kevin – but it was Dad I looked up to, it was Dad I admired and I never tired of telling people he was a policeman. My mum's family were all lovely people and I loved them to bits, but I also wanted the life my dad and stepmum enjoyed. They had good careers, a nice house, foreign holidays. I looked up to my stepmum too. She had a career, shopped in central London and went to the gym to keep fit, which in the eighties was a relative novelty. Mum thought going to the gym was a waste of time, and as for central London, forget it! We'd moved again, to Essex, and Mum hated going 'up London', as she called it. So we had the same routine every weekend – we went round Aunty Anne's house on Saturdays and Nan's on Sundays for dinner – corned beef sandwiches, cockles, jellied eels, winkles and rollmops. I loved all that too, but I wanted to do things differently, I wanted new experiences and I was dying to go 'up London'.

It wasn't that my dad was particularly well off. In the first few years after the divorce he had very little money, so on the weekends he took me and my brother to the lido at Barking Park and afterwards he let me sit on his lap and 'drive' his car round and round the car park. It was thrilling. Occasionally, he would take us to Deep Pan Pizza in Ilford – but this wasn't something he had the money for himself. I found out later it was free as part of the GTP (Good To Police) scheme. Afterwards, we'd drop by the police station to say hello to his work colleagues. The despatch controller was a matronly older lady called Maureen who sported gigantic red hair, electric-blue eye shadow and the deepest smoker's voice I'd ever heard.

'Come 'ere, darling! Come give your godmother a hug!' she'd growl in a voice so low and croaky it was painful to hear. But l loved her. And I ran into her arms for a great big squeeze that reeked of stale smoke. At the station everyone was really friendly and made a point of stopping to say hello, then Maureen would usher us into the tearoom at the back where she'd ply us with orange squash and terrible dry biscuits. Years later, when I took up my first posting in Tower Hamlets, one of the sergeants recognized me.

'I remember when your dad used to bring you to Ilford,'

he grinned. 'You'd have these lovely outfits on.' I cringed. I remembered those outfits too – white fur coat, white patent boots and massive gold hoop earrings. Yup, I was a proper little Essex girl through and through!

Dad steadily worked his way up through the ranks. When I was little, he was in uniform and one of the Advanced Response Drivers for his borough, which basically meant he was the cool cop that did all the fast car chases in BMWs. By the time I was studying for my A levels Dad had moved over to Crime Squad, which, in my view, was even cooler. For years I'd watched *The Bill* on ITV, believing it was exactly what my dad did. I suppose it was my way of feeling close to him when I couldn't see him, but I was also 100 per cent convinced the show was representative of real police work. Erm . . . it's not, by the way. But it was all I had to go on at the time. My favourite character was Polly Page – a young, down-to-earth police officer, Polly wore her blonde hair in a sensible, short bob and was feminine without being soft. Polly was a tough cookie from south London, a good, dedicated copper and committed to her job. Polly was cool. She was streetwise, smart and hard as nails. *I could be like that*, I thought, as I waited for my interview. *I could be like Polly Page.*

When the day of the interview came in 2002, I was really nervous, but Dad accompanied me to the Met's training college in Hendon with a bacon sandwich to eat en route, and I appreciated his reassuring presence as we entered the main building.

'Oh hi, Mark!' the officer behind the desk greeted my dad. Dad nodded back coolly as we walked past.

'He's such a cock,' he whispered under his breath.

'Dad! Don't say that!' I was mortified. I just hoped the Cock hadn't overheard. We walked through to the waiting room where Dad quickly left me to it and I took my place among the sixty other candidates interviewing that day, ready to be tested and grilled over several hours. Even from a quick glance I could tell I was the youngest by quite some way, still only eighteen. *I'll never get in*, I thought to myself as they outlined the structure of the day's tests. There was to be written exams, a verbal interview, a maths test as well as observational tests. First up was the interview.

I walked into the room, tugging anxiously at the hem of my Next suit skirt, only to be greeted by the Cock. *Oh god!* My cheeks flushed and I tried to compose myself. *Come on, Dan. This is no time to get embarrassed.* I had to get on with it. The questions were quite straightforward at first, all the standard things you'd expect to be asked in a job interview, like: Why do you want to join the police force? What skills do you bring to the job? What are your weaknesses? But gradually the questions got trickier and more theoretical.

'So, Danielle, tell me how you would deal with someone who is being very confrontational.'

I obviously had very little life experience at this stage, nothing to fall back on but my Saturday job. So I did the best I could.

'Probably the same way I deal with difficult customers in the store,' I replied with a confidence I didn't possess. 'I had this lady the other day, she was really angry. She brought back this chicken, saying it was off and was really

making a big stink about it. So I just talked to her, I asked
her how she could tell and she told me it smelled really
bad. Then I explained that she could exchange it and we
were sorry and we were grateful she'd brought it to our
attention. That calmed her down. Just being really composed,
listening to her, accepting what she'd told me rather than
challenging her.'

Really, Dan? Smelly chicken? Really? I could hardly believe
what was coming out my mouth and from this point onwards
I was pretty certain I was going home.

The maths exam was fairly basic so I didn't have any worries
about that. Afterwards we took the observational test, which
involved watching a video and then being quizzed on what
we had seen. This was where I actually did really well. I don't
know why, but I've always been hyper aware of my surroundings. Wherever I am, I'm always scanning the room, taking
in small details, making a mental note of everything going
on around me. If I'm in a cafe or bar, for example, I can't sit
with my back to the room, I have to look outwards so I can
see what's going on. So while most people focused on the
narrative of the video we were watching, I noticed all the
peripheral information. And when I was asked: 'What colour
coat was the lady on the bus wearing?' or 'What number bus
did she get on?', I had the answers.

It was a long day and at the end we were split into two
groups. My group was slightly smaller, of about twenty, and
was led into a small side room. Since I was the only woman
there, I guessed we were the rejects.

'Congratulations!' said the Cock, smiling broadly. 'You've

all passed the interview stage for the Met and we'd like to offer you all places on our next training course.'

Oh my god. I passed! It was quite a shock, especially since that meant around a dozen female candidates had failed to get in. *That's weird*, I thought. *I'd come for an interview during a drive to recruit more women and had been the only successful female candidate.* Still, I didn't think too hard on it. Dad was totally made up when he came to meet me afterwards.

'That's brilliant,' he said. 'Well done, love. I knew you'd do well. Are you going to take it?'

'Yeah, I think I am,' I smiled. I was going to be a police officer. I was going to be the real Polly Page.

I arrived at Hendon police training HQ on a cold Monday morning in February 2003, excited to be starting my new career. Most of the new recruits had arrived the night before but I was a late replacement when someone failed to show up for the course. Training was to last eighteen weeks and we all had to live onsite in the blocks of flats reserved for cadets. It was my first time away from home and I have to say my heart sank slightly when I moved my suitcases into my room. It was a soulless small bedroom with a metal sink, single bed, wardrobe and a desk. That was it. I shared a laundry room and communal showers with the other recruits. Sharing showers was my idea of hell. *Oh well, it's only for a few months*, I thought cheerily as I unpacked my clothes and made my bed. That first night, I wandered nervously into the bar, keen to make a few friends. Luckily, the place was filled with other nervy-looking new recruits like me and we soon got chatting. I felt slightly out of my depth being so young and fresh out of school. There were university graduates here and others who had come from different professions. And, a LOT of men! Of the thirty on our course there were only six women – luckily, me and two other new recruits got on famously right from that very first night and from that point on I knew I'd found two great friends.

'Can I get a skirt please?' I asked brightly as I stood at the desk of the uniform store the next morning. First things first; I needed to be kitted out.

'Sorry, love, we don't have any skirts,' the bored-looking store clerk replied. I was crushed.

'No skirts?'

'Nope, most of the women wear trousers. We can order one for you, if you like, but it might take a bit of time to get here.'

'Yes please – can I do that?' I gave him my measurements and in the meantime he did his best to gather uniform in my size. It wasn't easy – at just over five foot and seven stone, I was clearly not the average-sized copper. The trousers were massive, reaching all the way up to my belly button, I got lost in the cavernous vests and my hat wobbled comically on my head. It was so big I could fit all the fingers on both hands under the sides. I felt like a young kid playing dress-up with her dad's uniform. In the end, Mum helped me out, getting handy with a needle and thread to make my uniform fit. And eventually they sent me a skirt which I proudly wore for parades and ceremonial events.

The parades took place every day – mostly, so far as I could see, for the instructors to check your uniform. The first few occasions were really weird. No one had told us what to do so we just guessed as we went along. There was a small man with a squashed face shouting orders at the front and we did our best to keep up: 'STAND TO ATTENTION. ON THE LEFT . . . AND QUICK MARCH!'

Mr Squashed Face was actually really mean and I noticed over time that he liked to pick on the girls. If you weren't completely pristine he'd make an example of you, showing you up in front of the rest of the group. The main issues were seemingly hair-related. If it wasn't pulled back really tight into a bun at the back of your head without a single, flyaway strand you'd be 'show paraded'. This meant that on the next parade you would have to march alone, out in front of the class so everyone could see you. Horrible!

I teamed up with two other girls I'd met in the bar on the first night and we quickly became best mates. We all had nicknames – I was Dinky (for obvious reasons), Louise was Three Bellies and Lisa, the Arse. Collectively we were known as the Three Witches, because once one of us started laughing, the other two would crack up and then we'd just be sat there, cackling like a coven. It was an intense course but together we had the best time. Every Friday we were tested on what we'd learned that week, whether it was traffic offences, writing out an accident book, or taking the fitness tests. There was even a test to see how we'd react to getting sprayed with CS. Badly, as it happens! That stuff really makes your nose snot and eyes sting and you think it's all over but then you get in the shower and the particles come out of your hair and into your face and set you off again. Still, we all had such a laugh together, playing pranks on each other and winding up the course leaders. We took it in turns to write out traffic violation tickets and stick them on our tutor's moped and he never suspected it was us!

For me, Hendon was like going to university. Sure, I learned a lot about police work, but most of all, I had a great time making new friends and learning something of the outside world. Until this moment I'd lived a pretty sheltered life, growing up in Dagenham, doing the same things every weekend, even dating the same boy in high school since the age of twelve. We were Daniel and Danielle – so corny! He was captain of the cricket and football teams and I was the model student. He was a lovely boy but I was quickly learning there was a lot more to life than what Dagenham had to offer. If we weren't at the bar on campus, my friends and I were mixing with the military at the Claddagh Ring in Mill Hill on Sunday nights, hopping up to Nottingham or Liverpool for the weekends or heading into the West End for a spot of clubbing. Daniel wasn't happy.

'Why don't you want to come home and see me this weekend?' he moaned when I told him I wasn't coming back for the fourth weekend in a row. Eventually, I realized we'd reached the end of the road and told him it was over between us. Now I was free to live my own life and I made the most of it.

Mum came up to see me every Sunday evening, bringing fresh bedsheets and filling up my fridge for the week ahead.

Even though she hadn't been keen on my joining the force in the first place, she was brilliantly supportive once I got in. The entire group of new recruits helped each other out as well. We formed small study groups each week to test each other on that week's subjects, determined nobody would fall behind. It was a real collective effort. We had to score over 70 per cent on each test and pass at least twelve out of eighteen tests to successfully complete training. Of course, once I was out on the streets, I discovered that the stuff we were taught in Hendon bore very little resemblance to real police work. There were tests on fog lights, for example, and nothing about sexual offences. It was all very theoretical – getting to grips with the difference between burglary 9a and 9b, for instance – but for the really important stuff, we had to learn on the job.

Towards the end of the course we were asked to choose the borough for our first postings, listing our preferences in order, and I was thrilled when I found out I got my first choice of Tower Hamlets. Since I was born in Mile End, in the borough of Tower Hamlets, we had lots of family there and I knew it well. It was busy, cosmopolitan and, like many parts of London, extreme wealth and extreme poverty sat side by side. This meant there would be plenty of crime to get stuck into and even though I wasn't sure yet what I wanted to do, I knew one thing: I did not want to spend my time on the force writing traffic tickets! Nevertheless, it was a sad day when me, Three Bellies and the Arse all had to say our final goodbyes as we left Hendon to take up our first posts in different boroughs. We attended our passing-out parade, hugged tightly, vowed to stay in touch and got drunk together one last time. I'd passed Hendon and now I was keen to start work and prove myself as a really good copper.

2

Thief Taker

'Isn't that Mo Habidi?' I nodded towards a man in a long, charcoal-grey trench coat standing on the corner of the street, pulling on a cigarette in a cupped hand. In the other he held something black and mechanical. I instantly recognized the man's face from the daily briefings. It was my first week on the job and after we'd been introduced to borough command, we were shown how to use the intelligence systems and given our shoulder numbers – mine was 379HT – before we were sent out on street duties with experienced officers. I was so excited as I arrived at Brick Lane Market on Sunday morning – the place was buzzing with activity and, aside from the usual market bustle, it was clear there was a ton of dodgy stuff on sale. This place was a known hot spot for stolen goods, particularly bikes, and we'd only been walking for about ten minutes when I spotted him: Mo Habidi. Mo was a PromNom – Prominent Nominal – which meant he had been arrested a number of times. I walked a little closer just to be sure – yes, he had that very distinctive mole on his right cheek.

'It's him,' I confirmed to my senior officer. 'Shall we go and speak to him?'

We crossed the street and headed towards Mo. As we got closer I could see that the black box he was clutching was actually a car radio.

'Hello Mo,' I said. 'It is Mo, isn't it?'

'Yeah – what do you want?'

'Whose car radio is that?' I asked.

'It's mine.'

'Really? Do you own a car? Do you hold a driving licence?'

Mo stared off into the distance, pretending he hadn't heard, and my partner frowned. I used my personal radio to check back with the CAD (Control Aided Despatch) operators. The CAD operators receive all the calls funnelled down to the borough and send out the appropriate response teams. It turned out that Mo had been disqualified from driving some months back.

'You're disqualified, Mo, which means you don't have a car,' I said. 'So tell me, why have you got a car radio? Is it yours?'

Mo shrugged. This was a no-brainer. He was handling what was almost certainly a stolen radio. I really had no choice but to arrest him.

My first arrest! I can't pretend I wasn't a little nervous as I cautioned Mo and led him back to the police car. My partner stood back, letting me take the lead as he knew this was my first time. Once we were in the car, he said: 'Right, let's get him back to the station then. Good work, PC Brooke.'

I felt like such a big girl as I walked Mo into the station and handed him over to the custody sergeant. The senior officers in the station couldn't hide their surprise. After all, I'd been in service for just a matter of days.

'She's quick off the mark,' one remarked.

'A proper thief taker,' the constable nodded. 'The rest of the probationers have barely got their boots out the station. Well, Brooke, your first arrest!'

I was pleased as punch. But then, just as I was giving my account to the custody sergeant, a CID detective wandered past the front desk. He squinted in our direction.

'Is that Mo Habidi?' he asked.

'Yes, sir.'

'You brought him in?'

'I did, sir. Suspected of being in possession of stolen goods.'

'Fantastic,' he grinned. 'We've been wanting to speak to him for ages. He's wanted for a number of offences. It's okay, PC Brooke. We'll take it from here.'

I've got to admit it was a little galling handing over my first arrest to CID but then I suppose just getting him into the station was good. My first custody number! Little did I realize, Mo Habidi would turn out to be the bane of my existence over the next few years, our paths crossing on many occasions. He was always hanging around, doing something stupid and usually arrestable!

There was no question, I was keen. As the new borough intake we weren't generally expected to do much in those first six weeks on the job other than make the tea and toast. Our 'babysitting' officers were all very nice cops but they didn't think we'd be making arrests straight away. Tower Hamlets consisted of five teams with around twenty-one officers on each team. We worked in eight-hour shifts – either from 6 a.m. till 2 p.m., 2 p.m. till 10 p.m. or 10 p.m. till 6 a.m. – but at first, all the new officers on probation like me were given day duties. We were stationed as a 'uniformed presence' on the streets rather than tasked with taking on any active crime, and we walked everywhere. For one whole week, for example, I found myself assigned to the 'school kick out', which just meant standing outside the large Catholic school in Tower Hamlets to stop any 'trouble'. In theory, we were there to prevent public order offences. We didn't, of course. In reality, the kids who wanted to fight or get up to anything illicit could just go round the corner, away from where we were standing, and do it there.

Standing around in a uniform just to 'be seen' was not my idea of real police work. I wanted to prove myself and I wanted to get involved as much as possible, talking to people, getting to know the borough, making arrests. I'll never forget travelling in the van during my first blue-light run. One of the officers on our team called in for assistance and we all jumped in the nearest vehicle and headed to his location. It was so cool. I loved the adrenalin rush of driving at speed, the noise, hanging on to your seat as the van careered around bends. It was thrilling. The next day I told my mum: 'We went in the blue lights last night.'

'Well, I hope you wore your seatbelt. I hope you were safe.'

I grinned. That was just like my mum! I was out busting criminals on the mean streets of Shadwell and she was worried about whether I was wearing my seatbelt.

There was the odd late shift during the first six weeks of 'street duties', for variety, but then once we were assigned our teams we were put on all the shifts, including nights, and we truly got a taste of everything. I enjoyed it all, even being the 'gaoler' in the custody cells. Most new recruits found it boring – taking the prisoners down to the cells, monitoring them, giving them food and drink. But I really liked the chance to talk to the prisoners and I had a lot of respect for the custody sergeant, who was amazing with them. He had a way of treating people with respect and kindness that calmed even the most agitated prisoner. Generally, if you were nice to them they were pretty nice back and occasionally they would open up to you in unexpected ways.

One night I was on gaoler shift taking care of a woman who'd been nicked for suspected murder. Since I was the only woman on duty that night it had been my job to strip-search her when she arrived. She wasn't your usual criminal type, to be honest. She was dressed in nice clothes, had an expensive-looking hairstyle and spoke well, as if she had been privately educated. But as she undressed I spotted several strange puncture marks surrounded by purple bruises around her groin area.

'What are those?' I asked, curious.

'Track marks,' she replied. I was so innocent I didn't know what she meant. I must have looked blank because she went on: 'It's where I inject.'

Again, I was mystified, and finally she sighed: 'Heroin.'

That blew my mind. She didn't *look* like a heroin addict, she didn't *act* like an addict. She looked and behaved like a smart, educated and together person. Of course, these days I know that addicts come in all shapes and sizes and there are plenty of long-term 'functioning addicts' like this woman, holding down jobs and maintaining their lives. Things had obviously taken a dark turn for her, though.

We got chatting and I asked her how she started using. She said it was the stress of life which led her to try it the first time, and from there she was always chasing that first high. It was so eye-opening. I never imagined people like her getting addicted to heroin. Later, she asked to go out for a cigarette and when we were sitting outside in the courtyard she said simply: 'I did do it.'

'What?''

'I killed him. The knife's behind the radiator.'

Oh my god. She's just confessed to murder. I could hardly believe it. I may have been new but I knew that this was not the way things normally went: *Fuck fuck fuck. What do I do now?*

'Well . . . erm, I think we better go back now,' I murmured and she obediently stabbed out her fag on the ashtray and stood up. All the way back to the cells my heart was racing. She'd just confessed, but I couldn't ask her any more questions – that was strictly prohibited. If she was going to be interviewed it needed to be done properly in an interview room with the tape recorder going. Besides, we were being watched by the station's CCTV system.

After I'd returned her to her cell, I made my way to the murder squad who were in the canteen.

'Erm, I need to tell you something,' I started nervously as I hovered by their table. 'The female murder suspect has just confessed. And she says she's hidden the knife behind the radiator.'

The look on their faces was one of pure shock. For a split second nobody moved or said anything. Then the detective inspector leaned forward, frowning: 'Are you joking, PC Brooke?'

'No,' I could hardly believe it myself. 'No, I'm not joking. It's all on the CCTV footage. I've been in custody with her all night. I took her out to the courtyard for a fag earlier and she said she did it and hid the knife behind the radiator.'

'Fuck me!' the DI exclaimed. 'Well, you better make a statement.'

It turned out the knife *was* behind the radiator, just like she said. I was nervous that I might have to go to court if she decided to plead not guilty. Fortunately, I was never called to give evidence so I guessed she had made up her mind to take an early plea in the hope of mitigating her sentence.

I quickly got a name for myself around the station as someone who made a lot of arrests, a 'thief taker', as the custody sergeant had said when I brought Mo Habidi in that first week. And it was true that my arrest rate was higher than all the other new officers on probation; higher, in fact, than most of the other officers in the station. I didn't hold back but, at the same time, things just seemed to happen when I was around. If there was trouble then I was bound to bump into it. *Am I a thief taker or a shit magnet?* I wondered to myself, especially after my experience at Notting Hill Carnival. That August, all of us new recruits were assigned to the carnival, which, like most Londoners, I saw as a colourful, benign feature of the capital's annual calendar. I had never seen the other side to it – the dark, criminal side – until I was drafted to police it.

The first day started early, with around thirty of us from Tower Hamlets meeting at the borough at 6 a.m. before boarding the coach to the main police centre for the carnival. There, we were given breakfast and a packed lunch and briefed by Bronze Command. All the intelligence was fed into a central command centre, which is led by a very high-ranking officer known as Gold Command and from there it was given out to command centres, led by a Silver Command officer, and then to a Bronze Command officer. It was then relayed to the ground inspectors who disseminated it to the officers on the ground. Next, we were deployed in pairs to police a particular area of the carnival for the next twelve hours, to act as 'walking uniforms', a 'presence', nothing more.

At first everything was hunky-dory. I was on patrol with another female officer from the station and we both took a relaxed attitude to the festivities. People were smoking weed everywhere and nobody cared. It was a class B drug in 2003, so technically we could have nicked them for it, but neither of us saw the point. We would have had to arrest half the street! We were just there to ensure there wasn't any trouble and everything went off smoothly. Tourists stopped to ask directions, we were offered joints and asked to dance, because apparently we were both '*fiiiine*'. Some even danced against us without our permission but it was all light-hearted and in good spirits. It was a long day, and towards the end of our shift we got word that things had kicked off.

'Here we go,' my partner sighed. She was three years in service so this was not her first carnival.

'What? What's happened?' I asked.

'Every year, every bloody year,' she shook her head. 'Gangs, knives, fights. It always happens!'

We strained to listen to our radios over the heavy bass of the sound systems – there had been a stabbing and the command had put a Section 60 in place. A Section 60 was a stop and search order designed to root out weapons in the area. It meant we were now required to stop and search people without grounds or suspecting them of any offence.

'I don't know why they don't just put the section sixty in place before the carnival,' my partner said. 'That might deter the gangs to start with if they knew the Old Bill was here, stopping everyone. The thing is, it always starts between the gangs and ends with an officer getting hurt.' I looked at my watch – it was 6.30 p.m. and we were half an hour away from the end of our brutal twelve-hour shift.

We were both so tired – all we could think about was the relief coming in so that we could go home and rest. After all, we were due to do this all again tomorrow. Nevertheless, an order was an order and we had no choice but to make the stops. I just hoped that the next half an hour would be uneventful. I started to stop people randomly, with no particular intelligence guiding my choice of punters, just hoping that whomever I stopped would be friendly enough not to give me any hassle. Ten minutes in, I spotted a guy in a gold bucket hat and a Gucci man bag sauntering down the road towards us, chatting to a guy in a pair of denim dungarees.

'Hi!' I said cheerily.

'Hello, Officer,' said the guy in the gold hat. He was

smiling and seemed really friendly. Mr Dungarees didn't say a word.

'You got anything on you you shouldn't have?' I asked.

'Yeah,' he smiled.

I laughed, thinking he was joking.

But he looked at me and suddenly I realized he was serious. *Oh no.*

My fellow officer, standing on the other side of the road, rolled her eyes at me. I was almost afraid to ask but I had no choice: 'So, what have you got on you then?'

'A knife.'

'No, you haven't!'

'I have. Look!' and he pulled a large knife from the back of his jeans.

Oh bollocks. That's all we need.

I took a deep breath and looked at the guy that I'd stopped. He seemed really nice and had been so friendly and cooperative, I wondered if he knew what he was doing. His friend was long gone.

'Look, mate, you know you're going to get nicked, don't you?'

'Yeah, but I thought I'd tell you because you were going to search me anyway.'

Well, he was absolutely right about that. I nicked him and took him to the prisoner processing centre in Charing Cross. And since my partner was the witnessing officer she had to come too. Worst of all, since we'd all come together from Tower Hamlets, the rest of the coachload of thirty officers had to wait for us to all get home.

At Charing Cross Police Station the queue to book in prisoners was over an hour long.

'You don't have to wait. We can get the tube back,' I said to my guvnor. After putting in twelve-hour shifts, I felt so bad for the rest of my team.

'No, we have to stay together,' she insisted.

It turned out Mr Gold Hat was wanted on a recall to prison for breaching his bail conditions. Finally, we booked him in, quickly submitted our reports and handed him over to the custody sergeant. I was kicking myself. *Why did I have to stop this guy?! I should have asked his friend in dungarees instead!*

To be honest, I wasn't that keen on policing the carnival. Despite the party atmosphere, for me it was long, boring and annoying, just standing around all day giving directions and being dry humped by excited dancers who liked the look of female cops. I didn't enjoy manning the front desk in the station either, dealing with people who had lost their wallets. Very occasionally you'd get someone bursting in with blood pouring from their head because they'd been involved in an accident or they'd been mugged and knew the police station was nearby so they'd run straight from the scene. But generally, it wasn't exciting police work. I preferred being on the streets, getting to grips with crime. And I learned so much from working with experienced officers.

One 'domestic' in particular stood out in my mind for taking a disturbing twist. We'd taken a call from a neighbour who had overheard what he called a 'violent row' next door, so me and another officer called Mick went to investigate.

Mick was a great officer, he had loads of service and was really knowledgeable. His instincts were usually spot on and I always learned a lot when we were sent out together. Back then, there weren't the same protections in place for victims of domestic abuse as there are today and generally these call-outs wouldn't usually end in arrest unless we saw evidence of a physical assault. The standard way of dealing with 'domestics' in those days was to split the couple up, keep them apart until they'd both calmed down. We'd send the wife to her mum's house and insist the fella stay put. But this time, it was different.

'All right, mate,' Mick said to the bloke who opened the front door of the end-of-terrace semi. 'We've had a report of a violent disturbance at your property. Do you mind if we come in?'

The man seemed surprised to see us but he was calm and in control of himself.

'Yes, me and the wife did have a barney,' he said. 'But it's fine now. It's all sorted.'

He kept the door open just a crack as he spoke to us, clearly not pleased with our presence.

'Okay, well, we're going to have to come in,' said Mick, putting a hand on the door.

'Yeah, sure,' said the man, stepping back and opening the door wide for us to enter.

We walked in and were shown through to the lounge. Everything appeared normal and in order. There were no obvious signs of distress or damage, he had no cuts or scratches, but I had a feeling something wasn't right.

'Sir, where's your wife?' I asked.

'Gone to her mum's. That's what she always does after a row.'

I had no reason to disbelieve him but still, I couldn't shake off an uneasy sense about this guy. We stayed about ten minutes but then, just as we were about to leave, I saw a bright-red spot of blood on the radiator in the corridor. Silently, I pointed it out to Mick.

I turned to face the man.

'Where is she?' I asked again.

'I don't know,' he said.

'You just told us she was at her mum's. Now you're saying you don't know . . .'

'Mate, just tell us where she is because there's blood and it's clearly not yours,' Mick added.

The man clammed up so we started to search the house, going from room to room, pulling open cupboards, looking under furniture. I walked upstairs into the master bedroom and what at first sight appeared a lumpy unmade bed, on closer inspection turned out to be the outline of a body. I whipped back the duvet and underneath there was a woman, completely unconscious.

I put my head to her chest. She was breathing okay.

'Hello? Hello, can you hear me? Can you wake up?'

Mick called the ambulance while I put her into the recovery position and she was like that for a good few minutes before she came round. She seemed dazed. It turned out he'd whacked her and she'd hit her head on the radiator, falling unconscious. When we'd turned up he'd panicked and put her in bed with the duvet over her. Thank god she was alive! We arrested him, of course, and she was taken straight to hospital to be checked for concussion. He was charged with assault and Mick went to court to give evidence. I was astonished when Mick returned with the surprising news that they were back together and she had refused to give evidence against him. Thankfully, he was convicted on the strength of our statements, but it gave me the chills to think what he might do to her next.

Domestic violence was a difficult and often more complex crime than I had previously imagined. Other than fear, there could be compelling reasons why women shielded their abusers and I found it very frustrating when we were called to a domestic incident only to find the victim wouldn't say a word to us. Or lied to protect the perpetrator. This was particularly true among the many Bangladeshi families in our borough, where we saw overwhelming evidence that the wife was getting hurt. They were terrified, these women, and wouldn't say a word because they knew there would be consequences for them – and their families – if they dared to speak. Many didn't speak English, and it was even worse if they lived with their husband's family because the threats came from multiple individuals. I desperately wanted to help these women escape, but where could they go? We didn't have the answers in the police service. All we could offer was the protection of the law and sometimes that just wasn't enough.

Working as an officer in Tower Hamlets really opened my eyes to what was happening on the streets, in people's homes, and in communities I'd never had any dealings with before. I was learning all the time, particularly about the places we were not welcome. There was one Traveller site in Bow which we were ordered to avoid as they hated the police and if you dared to drive onto the site, you would be attacked verbally and sometimes physically, with bottles pelted at the car. We could only go down in numbers or with TSG (Territorial Support Group, nicknamed the Thick and Stupid Group among officers). However, while I was a probationer, there was an operation to locate and seize a consignment of stolen caravans. At 6 a.m. one morning, fifteen of us went down to the site to make a note of all the chassis numbers on the bottoms of the caravans. If any were found to be stolen we would take them. Well, that didn't go down well! The Travellers started arguing vehemently for us to leave but they didn't have any choice in the matter. In the meantime, the guvnor turned to me: 'Danielle, you're the smallest. You're going under to read the chassis numbers out.'

I had to crawl under each caravan to read all the numbers out. We found one stolen caravan and the man living there with his family was arrested. He didn't come willingly and started to fight back. They all did, in fact! The whole site erupted in furious protestation. Even this guy's daughter, who couldn't have been more than five years old, screamed out: 'GET YOUR FUCKIN HANDS OFF MY FUCKIN DADDY!'

I only went back one other time to that site and it was on an urgent assistance call when a large-scale fight broke out. All units were called to assist, so we jumped in the cars and pegged it to the site. When we got there the whole place was brawling. About forty people – including women and children – were shouting, smacking each other, smashing and throwing stuff and attacking each other with literally anything they could get their hands on. There were knives, axes, bottles, even their dogs were wading in – it was carnage. And they weren't going to stop just because the Old Bill turned up. I spotted one guy in his mid-twenties, who was bleeding heavily from a wound in his thigh, army-crawling on his elbows to get back among the action. I squatted next to him.

'Mate, you need to stop,' I said with some urgency. 'You're bleeding really heavily – we've got to get you to hospital.'

'FUCK OFF!' he shouted. The smell coming off his wound was horrific – iron and musty – but I tried to sit on him and put pressure on the wound to stop him bleeding out. Another officer joined me as we wrestled to keep him still.

'GET OFF!' he yelled.

'STOP MOVING!' I shouted back. 'You're really injured. You're going to die or lose your leg if you don't get seen to straight away.'

We managed to get him into an ambulance and he remained angry with us the whole way. Once at the hospital, I stayed with him because we had no idea if he was a suspect and he would definitely have left otherwise. But he didn't speak to us – nobody from the site spoke to us – so we couldn't establish what had happened. I sat there, in the hospital, covered in this guy's blood, stinking to high heaven. There were no convictions on the back of that massive fight but at least we'd saved this guy's life.

It was rare for anyone to come willingly, but I didn't let my five-foot two height stop me from making arrests. If someone wasn't prepared to submit then I wasn't afraid to use force. One Friday night on Brick Lane, I had to arrest a drunk for a public order offence and he got right in my face, so I punched him in his. His eyes widened in surprise. *Yeah, you weren't expecting that, were you?*

'I will hit you again,' I warned as he staggered backwards. 'Get out of my face.'

It was completely justified. Back at the station, when writing up my notes, I put that I had 'felt in fear of my own personal safety'. The phrase was a cliché and a morbid joke among officers. 'Feeling in fear of your personal safety, mate?' was the standard jibe, because it was frequently the justification we wrote in our notes, also called our IRB (Instant Report Book), whenever an officer used force. For a 'short arse' like me such force was essential. I needed to be able to act swiftly to minimize my chances of getting hurt. We were often called out to break up fights at weddings – just drunk people being drunk – and though we all had asps (batons), I rarely used mine. Instead, I'd use a heel palm strike to the jaw to shock them enough to get one cuff on. Then, I could twist that cuffed arm up and around their back to get the second on. They hardly had time to react from the shock of the jaw strike before I had them neatly trussed up in cuffs. Job done! I may have been small but I was never scared. Not in my uniform. I had a job to do and the uniform was my protection. In it, I felt invincible.

3

Hidden in Plain Sight

After my first six weeks on street duties, I was assigned to the borough's Team E. No longer on the nursery slopes of street duties, we were now real cops, fully paid-up members of the force, and I was eager to get out there and prove my mettle. I was like a giddy kitten, taking every job and all the overtime I could, volunteering for every crappy job going. If there was a guard shift needed for a prisoner in hospital, I'd go. If a crime scene needed attending, I'd put my hand up. I was completely 'job pissed', meaning I was so wedded to the job it was like being drunk on police work. I loved it. No two days were the same. And even when things got tough – there were plenty of times I felt more like a social worker than a police officer – it was all part of a steep but amazing learning curve. We had to deal with everything and everybody, even those in crisis, people who had come to a point in their lives when they felt so bad they were ready to take desperate steps.

One day the call came in for units to respond to the Texaco garage on Cotton Street, where a man had doused himself in petrol and was threatening to blow himself up. Ours was the first car on the scene.

'Don't come any closer,' a tall, bald man in his thirties warned as I approached him on the station forecourt. He stood right next to the petrol pump, clutching a Clipper lighter, his eyes wild. He was very thin, his grey T-shirt and jeans were soaked in petrol and he was very agitated and shaky.

'I'm going to blow us all up, I'm going to kill us all,' he whispered, desperation in his voice.

'Okay, okay . . .' I said calmly. 'What's your name? I'm Danielle.'

'Simon. I'm Simon.'

'Hi Simon – why don't you—'

'DON'T GET ANY CLOSER! I'M GOING TO DO IT. I'M GOING TO DO IT. I'VE HAD ENOUGH.'

'Come on, this isn't going to help. You're going to hurt all of us as well and I know you don't want to do that, do you?'

'No, I don't. I just want it all to be over, so go away.'

'This is not the answer. Please let me help you. Please, Simon.'

'NO! You lot always say that but you never help me. You *never* help me.'

It was the first time I'd dealt with anyone so distressed. It was horrible, to be honest, but I didn't back down. We carried on talking and Simon told me about how he'd lost his mum to cancer a year earlier and had been drinking heavily since. He had nobody now and his mental health had got so bad he didn't want to live any more.

'Just give me the lighter,' I urged. 'I promise I won't leave you, Simon. I'll help you.'

He didn't trust me at first but I kept talking to him and

eventually he rolled the lighter to me. The immediate danger was over.

'Come on – come to me,' I said gently, beckoning him with outstretched hands. 'Let's sit down and have a chat.'

All the energy seemed to drain out of him and his body slumped forward as he walked towards me. We hugged and then walked back to the waiting police car together and sat down.

'We're going to have to take you to the hospital,' I explained. He needed to be sectioned, for his own safety.

'I don't want to go there. All they do is give tablets. I don't want to go. I really don't.'

'It's okay, Simon. I'll be with you.'

At the hospital in Newham it took over four hours to find him a bed. I held his hand the whole time, some comfort and reassurance in a world that seemed to have overwhelmed him. He may have been a grown man but he seemed like a lost child to me. Back at the station, after I'd changed out of my petrol-covered uniform, the guvnor awarded me a borough commendation for taking charge of a difficult situation and showing compassion to a person in crisis. It had been a tough day but, according to more experienced officers in our borough, this wasn't the first time Simon had threatened to take his own life. And it wouldn't be the last.

It was a few months later when the call came through on the radio: 'Man with knife says he's going to kill himself. He's asking for Danielle.'

I knew immediately who it was. 'Three-seven-nine we will take that. It's Danielle Brooke. It's Simon, isn't it?'

'Yes, it's him.'

This time he was at home, a tiny fourth-floor council flat in a tower block in Poplar.

'Thank god they've sent you,' he said when I walked in. The place was a wreck – peeling wallpaper, filthy carpets and empty bottles on every surface. Simon was holding a long breadknife in his left hand.

'Simon, how are you? What's going on?'

'They're not helping me. They're not doing what they said.'

'Okay, well, let's talk. But first, give me the knife because I'm scared and you don't want me to be scared, do you?'

'No, girl. No. No, I don't.'

He handed me the knife. Somehow I had to get him out of the flat because we weren't allowed to section him in his own home. I suggested we move outside but he refused, knowing very well we would section him there.

We sat down on the sofa together and started talking but something caught my eye – a spreading crimson stain on the bottom of his T-shirt.

'What you got under your T-shirt, Simon?'

'Nothing.'

'You can't lie to me, remember, because we're friends and friends don't lie to each other.'

I lifted up the bottom of his T-shirt to find several more knives tucked into the waistband of his jeans. When he'd sat down the point of one of the knives had dug into his skin and he was now bleeding.

'I can't sit here with you like that,' I said. 'I need all the weapons.'

It took some time to calm him down and in the end we managed to get him outside but he didn't want to be sectioned and there was a bit of a scuffle as we tried to get the cuffs on him. It was for his own safety but I couldn't help feeling sorry for him. Poor Simon. Whatever his mental health problems, he was right about one thing – he wasn't getting the help he needed. Several years later we met again; this time he was threatening to jump out of a skylight. That didn't even make sense. I don't know how anyone jumps out of a skylight. He'd asked for me by name and by coincidence, when I arrived on the scene, my cousin Rachel, a paramedic, was also there. We greeted each other with surprise.

'Danielle!' Simon shouted and waved from the skylight when he saw me.

'Do you know him?' Rachel asked.

'Yeah – we go way back.'

'This is my cousin – Rachel!' I shouted back up to Simon.

'Ah that's nice.' He was so happy to see us both that he almost forgot what we were all doing there! This time I let Rachel take Simon because she was on her way back to hospital. It was all over within about half an hour and I think it would have been much worse if he hadn't seen two familiar faces. Simon's case was tragic but not uncommon. It seemed to me that the care system was so chronically understaffed there just wasn't enough help available for everyone who needed it.

Around two months after joining Team E, our guvnor requested that me and a few other officers come in for our next shift in plain clothes. I really liked our guvnor. He had a sideline in leading search and rescue teams around the world and the stories he told about helping find survivors in the wake of disasters were fascinating. He was a very cool guy, the kind of person who inspired confidence and you felt you could talk to about anything. He didn't just do the minimum. You could tell he really cared about us all as individuals, as well as the team. He wanted us to be the best team in the borough.

The next day I came in wearing skinny jeans and a pair of battered Converse. I had seen other officers go out in plain clothes and thought it was quite cool, so I was thrilled. My friend Natalie wore cut-offs, a vest top and sandals.

'What have you come as?' the sergeant asked her.

'What do you mean? The guvnor told us to wear our own clothes today,' she replied.

'You're doing police work, not hanging out at the beach,' he shot back. 'You can't patrol in sandals. Go and find some proper shoes.'

I know we were young and naive but even I could see that her footwear was ridiculous.

Then he turned to me: 'You look like you're going on a night out.'

I was disgusted.

'Excuse me, I'm from Essex,' I replied huffily. 'As if I'd go on a night out in crappy jeans and Converse!'

I was posted with a South Asian copper called Mustapha – Taff for short. That first night without uniform was a revelation. We just looked like an ordinary couple on a night out, and nobody batted an eyelid. At first we had been given a

CID car – a battered blue Ford – but we parked up in Shadwell Gardens and decided to take the rest of the patrol on foot. It was incredible. There were people serving up in stairwells, groups of kids selling hot gear, prostitutes taking punters and all sorts of other stuff, but nobody cared that we could see them. We were right in among it and we started nicking people left, right and centre. Since it was such a success, the guvnor sent us out in plain clothes over and over again. That ruffled a few feathers, especially among the gangs, who thought they were safe from the Old Bill. We'd casually saunter towards a group acting suspiciously in a known drug-use area, shout 'Police, don't move!' and a whole group of them would starburst in front of you. Usually, we'd manage to nick at least one person in that group and that could lead to a lot of excellent intelligence. Our arrest rates went through the roof.

'Bloody hell, Dan, that's your fourth CRIMINT today!' exclaimed Natalie during one shift as I sat tapping away at the computer. 'You better finish up, cos we've got training in two minutes.'

'I know, I know,' I said. 'Just one more . . .'

The police intelligence system was known as CRIMINT – short for Criminal Intelligence. It was pretty archaic but it was our go-to resource. You could go in there and look up anything and anyone, like a Wikipedia for crime. Gathering intelligence was part of our job and we were all expected to input at least one or two CRIMINTs a day. It looked good, too, if the guvnor saw your team had inputted a lot of CRIMINTs during the shift. I loved CRIMINT and I looked stuff up on it all the time. Plus, being in plain clothes helped me source lots of great intelligence. I certainly didn't relate to the old police saying: 'A good copper never gets wet', meaning they know where all the good coffee stops are so they can hide out if it starts to rain. That seemed like a really weird attitude to me. Criminals don't stay in because it's raining! I'd rather get wet.

'Come on!' Nat dragged me out of my chair and we went through to the training room.

It turned out to be our most boring training session to date. They had just moved the missing person's reports from paper to an online system called N-Calt. N-Calt was notoriously slow and frustrating. You had to go through each page methodically and, even if it took you thirty seconds to answer the question, you still had to wait three minutes before it allowed you to move to the next page. I was about to doze off when a voice jolted me out of my reverie.

'Hi there,' it was a young, good-looking copper.

'Hi,' I said.

'Are you . . .?' he pointed at the screen.

'Yeah. Death by N-Calt!'

'We've got it next week for Team C. I'm Tom, by the way.'

'Hi. Danielle.'

'Can I take you out for a drink, Danielle?'

'Er . . . when?'

'Later?'

'Okay.'

Soon after passing my training course at Hendon, I'd managed to buy my own two-bedroom flat in Brentwood,

Essex with my savings, so we arranged to meet at a pub near there after our shifts ended, but the N-Calt session overran and by the time I got there I was nearly an hour late. It was a bit weird, to be honest. I hadn't been on a date in . . . well, forever! Daniel and I had started seeing each other when I was twelve and I hadn't been on a date since we'd split up. I had recognized Tom from the courses ahead of mine in Hendon. He stood out because he was tall but we hadn't spoken since joining Tower Hamlets. I sipped my Coke (I was driving) while Tom and I made tentative small talk. *He could have made more of an effort*, I thought, noting his trainers. In those days trainers were not considered proper footwear and in Essex we cared about that sort of thing. Tom told me he shared a house with four other officers, which wasn't at all impressive. But he seemed like a good guy, spoke nicely and when he asked me out again I said yes. Gradually, over the next few months, we became a couple. I hadn't really done 'dating' before now as I'd been with the same boy my whole time in high school, so it felt nice to be going out for dinner, to the cinema and even on holiday together. He was a little older than me too, I was still only nineteen, so I was flattered to be treated to meals out and he seemed very sophisticated, drinking red wine, which was something I'd never really come across before now. Everyone I knew drank alcopops and cider or lager. He appeared very grown up and mature, to my mind!

My horizons were being expanded on the job as well as off it, as I built and learned to navigate relationships with my colleagues on the force. On the whole, I really liked my team at Tower Hamlets. Our guvnor fostered great relations and everyone was friendly enough, though in time I found there were certain people I didn't enjoy being deployed with – like Dangerous Dan, for instance. He was a nice man, Dan, but he made stupid mistakes. One night when we were on patrol together, a call came through on the radio.

'Welfare check. Sixteen Smith Street. Who can respond?'

I was the operator that night, while Dan was driving.

'We're on it,' I replied and Dan drove us to Smith Street. It wasn't urgent – we just needed to check on an old gentleman who lived alone and hadn't been seen outside his house for several days. Once we arrived, Dan got out the car and went to knock on the door of number fifteen.

I stopped him. 'Dan, it's sixteen.'

'It's fifteen,' he replied, adamant.

'No, it's sixteen,' I said firmly. 'If you don't believe me we can ring it in again. No point getting it wrong.'

'I'm telling you, it's fifteen,' he insisted. Back then there were no computers in the cars – we just had the radio – but it wouldn't have taken any time to double-check with the CAD operator. Dan, however, was certain. And since he had more service than me, I couldn't do a lot to stop him. He went ahead and smashed down the door of number fifteen, only to find a very surprised family inside. That got him into a bit of trouble and I avoided being deployed with him after that. Dan had his own issues going on which could have contributed to poor decision-making – hence, the nickname – but either way I didn't want trouble because of his arrogance.

On the team, I earned a reputation as a hard worker so I

didn't mind the banter about being a 'short arse' or getting called 'dolly'. It was all said in affection and I knew there was nothing malicious in it, though in the post-MeToo era it certainly sounds unacceptable. How quickly things have changed! The point is that we spoke to one another in a robust way but, from my point of view at least, I never felt diminished or undermined by the language. Colleagues respected one another and though I can't speak for everyone, I do believe ours was a very inclusive team. Whatever was happening – summer barbecues, birthday drinks, Christmas parties – everyone was invited. Old-school ex-military cops hung out with the large gay presence in our borough – the Gaffia, as they jokingly referred to themselves – and everybody was treated with the same respect. We even had one copper who transitioned to female during my time on Team E and we got on famously. I grilled her on her life-changing decision and she quizzed me on buying bras!

If I was on the late or night shift I liked to be deployed with Rob, the old copper who drove the prison van, pinging from prisoner pick-up to prisoner pick-up so we got to see a bit of everything. Rob liked to do things his way and there was no arguing with him. At the beginning of each shift he'd buy a pack of twenty JPS fags and steadily work his way through the packet. Then, at 4 a.m., after picking up the first editions of the papers from Wapping, he'd drive round towards Blackwall and sit in the van, overlooking the O2 Arena, reading every single word of the papers. That was the worst bit. I didn't much like sitting around, doing nothing, and I especially hated it coughing my lungs up in a van full of smoke. There was so much going on in our borough. We could have been cruising round Shadwell or Stepney in the early hours, catching burglars or drug dealers. With a bit of proactive police work, who knows what we could have achieved! But Rob just sat there in silence, puffing one fag after another, the window firmly closed while I breathed in his toxic fumes.

After several months working nights with Taff, it got to the point where I preferred being in my own clothes to being in uniform. We got such good results that we even got tapped up for borough initiatives like catching bike thieves or clamping down on illegal taxi touts. For the taxi job, we had to stand around in known hot spots in Bethnal Green, trying to attract illegal taxis. According to borough command, there were illegal touts who were actually registered sex offenders so we had to find and stop them. Looking back now, I wonder if that really was the case. All these initiatives cost money and the borough would have to had given a good reason to fund them. Sex offenders operating illegal cabs sounded plausible, but more likely the team had had complaints from licensed taxis who were losing business and wanted us to do something about it. The job, conducted jointly with Transport for London, was fairly straightforward. I stood on a street corner, trying to flag a minicab. Then, when I got in the front seat, Taff would get in the back and before the driver had a chance to pull away, we'd flash our warrant cards and ask to see their documents.

It was an easy job and I didn't consider it dangerous because there were two of us. However, on one occasion there was a bit of an iffy moment when the driver started to drive off before Taff had a chance to get in properly. I showed my warrant card while Taff started to climb in the back seat but the guy put his foot down in a panic when he realized we were cops and Taff had to shout for him to stop as he half hung out the door! The driver went to pull the handbrake up but it fell out of its casing and we kept going. It was all a bit crazy but Taff managed to clamber into the car before the guy finally pulled over and thankfully he wasn't hurt from the unintended stunt. It was an exciting moment on an otherwise straightforward job and we laughed about it afterwards. Later that afternoon, just as I was clocking off, I was approached by the guvnor.

'You need to get up to New Scotland Yard tomorrow morning,' he said seriously. 'You've got a ten a.m. meeting in SCD10. Wear your smartest suit.'

4

Test Purchaser

My heels clacked loudly against the stone slabs as I made my
way into the large New Scotland Yard building in Victoria,
but I could barely hear anything over the roaring in my ears.
Oh god, oh god, oh god. I'm in deep trouble. I had no idea
why the guvnor had ordered me here but I guessed it might
be because of the work that I'd been doing with Taff. *Have
we pushed things too far?* I wondered, mentally returning to
every single arrest we'd made in the last few months. *Has
someone made a complaint? Was I going to get the sack?* I'd
called Dad the moment I got home last night.

'Dad, the guvnor's ordered me up to the Yard tomorrow.'

'Where to?'

'I've got to go to SCD10.'

'Right, okay.'

'Dad, am I in trouble?'

'Don't worry, love. I'm not really in a position to say
anything but I'm sure you'll be fine.'

That was cold comfort. Dad hadn't given me any reason
to feel less worried so I put on my best navy 'court' suit and
white shirt and went into the Yard as I was ordered, my heart
pounding with fear. I showed them my warrant card and

walked through security, then I stepped into the elevator. I had no idea what SCD10 even stood for. I had quickly looked it up on our intranet the previous night, searching for some mention of it in the daily briefings. Each borough had briefings which changed every morning and night and you could read all of these on the system. But there was nothing, not a single mention of SCD10. Who were these people?

Arriving on the right floor, I was surprised to find that it was secure. *That's odd.* I'd been to Scotland Yard a couple of times before for briefings and, once past the front desk, you could usually walk around without going through any extra levels of security. Palms sweating, I pressed the buzzer on the door and when a grizzled-looking man came to answer I said: 'I'm PC Danielle Brooke, 379HT.'

'Hiya – I'm John,' the man replied in a thick Scottish accent. John had long dark-grey hair, three-day-old stubble and was kitted out in a shabby brown leather jacket and Levi's. Frankly, he didn't look like a copper at all. He walked me through to a small meeting room and we sat down.

'Danielle, do you know why you're here?' he asked.

'No.' I was scared, that's all I knew.

'Do you know what this office is?'

'No.'

'Have you ever heard of the SCD10 unit?'

'No.'

'It's the covert unit.'

'Oh . . . right.'

'Your guvnor wants me to have a chat with you about it – he thinks you should do the course.'

I didn't really understand what he meant because I thought that was what I had been doing all this time! Getting all my information from episodes of *The Bill* really hadn't helped my knowledge of policing. Until that minute, I had no idea there was a whole separate unit in the Met that carried out covert operations.

Sensing my confusion, John explained: 'We run a covert intelligence unit here and those who have shown some skill and aptitude are offered the chance to take the Test Purchase course, or TP course. It's the first level of covert work. Test purchasing basically means buying drugs off the streets and any other specialism you might have, for example any particular knowledge or skills with languages.

'Once you've passed the course the test purchasing is done ad hoc – as and when we need you – so it works around your other policing commitments. The next level up is known as Level One and officers who have shown particular strengths in covert work are invited to take the NUTAC course to become a Level One officer. Level One officers work undercover full-time and their work can often involve long-term, immersive operations. So, now you know what it is, do you want to do it?'

'Yeah, I do.'

Truth be told, I still didn't have any idea what he was talking about. All I knew was that I wasn't getting sacked – today! – and they were offering to train me to go undercover. It all sounded good.

'Right, well the next course will take place at Hendon in February – do you think you can do that?'

'Yes, if the guvnor will let me.'

I must have sounded so innocent! I had no idea how things worked at that stage. I had no clue that SCD10 outranked my borough command by quite some margin.

Back at home I called my dad and told him about the offer to take the Test Purchasing course.

'I said yes but I don't know if I'll be any good at it, Dad. I don't know what it's all about.'

'You'll be fine,' he said. 'They've asked you to do it because they think you're capable. I guess all that work in plain clothes has paid off. This is a pretty big thing, you know. Most officers go their whole careers and they're never given the chance to take the course. It's impressive they've tapped you up so soon in service. Just roll with it.'

Dad said we had a friend who was a Level One officer and said I should talk to him before taking the course. I couldn't believe it when he told me who it was. I had no idea he worked undercover. We spoke briefly on the phone before I left to start the course but he was reluctant to give me any details on what to expect.

'I can't say anything, because if I did it would be obvious you'd been briefed,' he explained. 'All I'll say is the point of this is to put you into situations you wouldn't normally be in and see how you cope. They are designed to exert pressure on you, so keep that in mind. Also, take a variety of clothes. You're not going buying drugs off the street in your best suit. Make sure you've got all your angles covered. And finally, think about everything that's being said to you.'

While I waited for the course to start I filled in the vetting forms. These were much longer and more detailed than the ones I'd filled in to join the force. This time round they wanted to know everything about me – my family, my financials, my personal history and anything that was out there on social media, although thankfully that was much more limited back then. It was very detailed – top-level vetting. The night before the course I locked myself in the bathroom wearing some of my oldest clothes and lit several cigarettes, puffing one after another to get the smell into my clothes and hair. Then I went through to the kitchen and fried bacon with the door shut, just to add to the foul stench. I'd already dried these clothes in a bin bag so by the time I finished they really reeked. I was covering my angles, making sure that if I was on the street, I could blend in. I didn't want them to sniff me out! The next day I was back in Hendon but instead of wearing a uniform I was now dressed casually in jeans.

On the first morning of the course, eleven trainees sat in a semi-circle – four women and seven men – with four instructors at the front. All the instructors, I noted, were white, middle-aged men. Fortunately I was sat at the end of the horseshoe so when we were asked to introduce ourselves I went last. I watched and listened as each person gave a little speech about themselves and then the instructors asked some searching questions. It was clear they had done their homework on all of us. It was clear too that everyone had more service behind them than I did. When it came to my turn I gave out a little information and they started to ask me if I knew certain people or had been to certain places. They named a pub in Dagenham that was really rough. I frowned.

'Yeah, I know it by reputation, but that's all,' I said. *Were they deliberately trying to trip me up?*

After this first round of introductions one instructor called Liam explained: 'We're going to be buying drugs on this course so it's important that you have good street knowledge. Maybe you or your friends have done drugs in the past. So we want to know – what do you guys know? What are your experiences?'

Alarm bells started to ring. A couple of people said that they had been around friends who had done drugs. I had certainly seen people doing drugs but I said something very general and vague about how it took place in clubs I'd been to. One guy was really open and admitted that he'd smoked puff and taken ecstasy when he was a teenager. The instructors were suddenly very interested in this guy and encouraged him to speak more, but inside I was screaming *STOP! DON'T SAY ANYTHING ELSE!* Sure enough, the next day that guy was gone.

That's what it was like the whole week – the instructors set little traps, then encouraged us to walk in and screw things up. People dropped like flies, so I had to keep my guard up the whole time. It got to the point where I was always 'alert', even sleeping with the lights on. Day after day we'd act out role-playing situations in front of the group, creating our 'legends' – back stories that would seem authentic out in the field. Who were we? What were we doing there? That was half the job – working out a viable legend that would withstand interrogation if anyone got nosey. In drama lessons at school I was too self-conscious to 'perform' in front of the rest of the class but in this instance, I didn't care what my fellow trainees thought. I went for it and in each situation I assessed what would be the best way to handle things, throwing myself in completely. Sometimes I watched how things panned out with the other candidates and if it went badly I made a mental note not to use that narrative or technique. One day I was asked to make a wrap for cocaine. Now I'd seen what wraps looked like and I knew how to make an envelope so I took a lottery ticket, tore off the end to make a square and made a very neat looking wrap. To be honest, I had no idea I knew how to do it until that moment! On another occasion we were shown packets of fake drugs and asked how much we'd pay for each. They explained that we needed to know if we were being mugged off. That same afternoon a bloke came in with real heroin and showed us how to cook it up. It was important for us to see how it was done and what it smelled like.

They certainly didn't make it easy and even when we were role-playing they made us spell out what we were asking for, listening to the way we spoke and the words we used. I'd spent a fair amount of time around crackheads on patrol in Tower Hamlets, and like anyone my age I knew people in my social circle took drugs recreationally, so I thought I knew the street slang. Still, I did my homework and even looked up various slang terms and narcotic effects of different drugs on the Frank website. It sounds silly now, but I reasoned that if this resource was available to help young people navigate the world of drugs, I didn't see why it shouldn't help me too. My Essex accent steadily turned more 'street' as the week went on and in the role-plays I heard myself using the words 'bruv' and 'geezer' more and more. If they wanted street, I was going to give it to them!

It appeared that one of the major pitfalls for a woman was avoiding the 'prostitute' narrative. You didn't necessarily have to identify yourself as a 'working girl' as such. It just seemed that any woman buying drugs for herself was at risk of being propositioned. And let's face it, if you're a desperate heroin addict and some dealer says he'll take a blowjob instead of cash, nine times out of ten an addict will opt for the blowjob and free drugs. If you didn't it would look suspicious. I was super conscious of this. Time after time I saw female candidates getting caught in this trap. I resolved never to let myself get backed into that particular corner so I said the drugs were for my boyfriend. I was determined not to fuck this up.

One by one, the trainees were sent home and everything became more intense. Now, instead of being able to watch a role-play with eight other trainees we were down to five. I didn't shower the whole week, I didn't even clean my teeth. If I was going to 'pass' on the streets I had to look, smell and seem the part. It wasn't the same as buying the odd pill in a club – anybody can be a recreational drug user, but to buy hard drugs off the streets you really had to become the part, otherwise you'd get sniffed out straight away and that would be that. There were no second chances. If you blew an operation it was all over, wasting tens of thousands of pounds of taxpayers' money on a covert job gone wrong. Becoming someone who could 'pass' on the streets – and doing it consistently – was known as 'field craft', and it was a big part of the course. So while I may have been an Essex girl who took pride in her appearance in normal life, I wanted to show these instructors that I could be the grubbiest candidate on the course. The commitment was total. It wasn't like we could clock off at 5 p.m. when our lessons seemingly came to an end for the day. We were with the instructors all the time, and one night Liam said: 'We'll go for drinks tonight. We're going to run up to Sainsbury's – what does everyone drink?'

Stupidly, I said red wine. The thing is – and I should have guessed from the start – this so-called 'social' was part of the test. For one thing they didn't ask us to chip in. If this was a social drink everyone would be putting something in the kitty. They didn't ask us for cash. Also, they didn't take us to the bar. There was a really good, cheap, subsidized bar at Hendon but we were shown to a back room where they started plying everyone with booze out of plastic cups. One guy belatedly tried to claim he didn't drink but that didn't wash, and soon they were going round refilling everyone's glasses at a furious rate.

Shit. They are trying to get us pissed! I wish I'd realized sooner because red wine has a really high alcohol content. I was all of seven stone and since I was hardly eating properly because of the stress of the course, it struck me I'd be smashed after the first glass. *I've got to do something or this will get very messy!* On the drinks table there was a choice of either polystyrene or see-through plastic cups. I grabbed a polystyrene cup and poured my drink into that. At least this way they couldn't see how much I was drinking. My plan worked for all of half an hour. These guys weren't stupid. Adam, one of the instructors, came up to me with the bottle of red wine, all ready to pour. But before he did he said: 'Give me that cup, Danielle!'

'What?' I acted dumb. 'Why? What's wrong with it?'

'Just give it here,' and he took it and poured the contents into a see-through cup.

'That's better,' he grinned wickedly. 'Now we can tell when you're running low.'

It was tricky to avoid the refills for the rest of the night but I took it as slow as I could, probably drinking only two glasses of wine in total. Others weren't quite so careful and once they had a few in them they started to get quite loose-lipped, fessing up to their drugs experiments when they were young or giving out information about their real police jobs, which they shouldn't have done. We were still being tested and giving out this kind of revealing information about our day jobs was a strict no-no. The trainers were all chatty and charming but the next day two more trainees were gone.

On the final morning we went into our meeting room to find a new face there. A really handsome face! This guy was off-the-scale good-looking. Mario was from Portugal, Liam explained, and was in the UK to observe the TP training with a view to implementing similar courses in Portugal. Everyone was checking him out, even the fellas. During the next role-play he took the part of the senior instructing officer, silently watching while Adam went over my statement for our fake 'court' appearance. Mario was the officer who signed my instructions for deployment. These are done before every job to make sure you fully understood the objective and mission. But I was so distracted by Mario I could barely concentrate on what was being said and when I was asked to sign I did it automatically, without looking properly.

We then role-played the court scene where each of us had to give evidence in the witness box to support the prosecution, defending the undercover work we'd workshopped for the past few days. About two minutes in, Liam, who was role-playing the defence barrister, held up the instructions I'd just signed.

'Can you read out the date on this form please?' he asked, handing it to me. I looked down and my heart sank. I'd failed to notice the date was wrong when I signed it.

'Erm, I've put the wrong date here,' I said straight away. 'I know it says December but it should say November. That's my mistake.'

'A mistake? PC Brooke, if you've made a mistake about the date, could it be you are mistaken about my client's guilt?'

'No, I'm not mistaken about that at all. It was just a stupid error. I'm sorry, I didn't see it until now.'

Damn. It was my own fault but I felt so humiliated as Liam ripped into my evidence. *Handsome Portuguese bastard!* I silently cursed the beautiful man watching us from the corner of the room. I couldn't believe I'd been caught out like this on the last day.

By the last session on Friday afternoon, me and another girl Nic were invited to go through to the back room, the fake bar where they had previously held our 'drinking session'. I thought it was all over and that I was being sent home. But when we opened the door, we were greeted by a group of smiling officers: John, Adam, Liam, the other instructors and a few active test purchasers (referred to as TPs) who we'd met at different points on the course.

'Congratulations, Dan and Nic!' said Adam. 'You passed the course. Welcome to the team!'

Nic and I looked at each other in shock – just the two of us?

'Seriously?' I asked.

'Don't look so surprised. You did great.'

Naturally, we were happy that we'd successfully made it through but I was stunned that out of eleven potential TPs, only two of us were left standing at the end. There had been some strong candidates and at least one other woman who I felt sure was a shoo-in. She even looked the part, bedraggled and skinny enough so you'd have no problem believing she had a drug habit. I was just relieved it was all over. It had easily been the most gruelling week of my life and I was at the end of my rope. I chucked down a plastic beaker of warm wine and it barely touched the sides.

'I thought I'd blown it when I put the wrong date on the rules form,' I admitted to Adam afterwards.

'Nah. You fessed up to your mistake straight away and that made a difference,' he explained. 'If you'd tried to cover it up or made excuses it might have been a different story. Honesty paid off.'

'So, that guy . . . is he really from Portugal?'

'No, he's from Haringey!' Adam laughed. 'We had to try to get you somehow.'

'Bastards!' I said, shaking my head.

I asked John what would happen next and he said that as soon as our vetting came through we would be deployed. So I went home and waited. I didn't tell Mum about the course because we'd been warned that the fewer people who knew the better. And I didn't want to burden my mum with that type of secret. I hadn't said anything to Tom either, because I didn't want it getting out among the other officers in Tower Hamlets. Dad was the only person I had confided in about taking the course and he was thrilled when I told him I'd passed.

'You know what this means, don't you?' he said. 'This is such a good career move.'

I think it's fair to say that the TP course changed me. Going through a week of assessment where people are trying to catch you out every second of the day and night is exhausting but it also makes you more aware. And though I was always tuned in to my surroundings, now I became hyper aware, assessing every situation all the time, trying to stay one step ahead. This was overthinking on a different level. I realized that being undercover in real life would be even more demanding, testing my skills and ability to think fast on my feet. And now that I'd trained for it I was keen to get out there and try it out in real life. So after a week sitting around, waiting for my vetting to come through, I called the vetting office.

'Sorry, love, there's a bit of a backlog here. It could be up to six weeks.'

'Six weeks?!'

What if I forgot everything I'd learned in that time? I couldn't wait six weeks. From that point I rang the vetting officer up every other day, checking on the status of my form, trying to hurry her along. I even got John to push from his end.

'We need to deploy this officer,' he argued. 'I've got jobs backing up here – can't you just put her form to the front of the queue?'

Poor lady. In the end I think we must have worn her down because my vetting arrived after two weeks. The next day John called me up: 'Dan, are you free tomorrow? I've got a little job for you.'

In Hendon, Nic and I had barely spoken because, well, I didn't trust a soul on that course. For all I knew she could have been a plant. But now that we had both qualified together – and survived the most gruelling week of our lives – we started to get to know one another. I called her the moment I found out I was going on a job.

'My vetting's through and I'm being deployed tomorrow!' I told her excitedly that night.

'Dan, that's great. Mine's still not through yet.'

'I've been hassling the vetting officer every day. I think she just got sick of hearing me whine at her.'

'Well, it worked. Good luck. Let me know how it goes.'

'I will.'

I was so excited I barely slept that night. A million possibilities went through my mind. Could I do it? How would I handle each situation? Though I was about to embark on my new life as an undercover officer, it was a total leap into the unknown. I had no real idea what I was getting into, the situations I'd be placed in, the sort of people I would end up mixing with or the new direction my life would take. I thought I knew what it was all about but, really, I didn't have a clue.

5

Bite and Run!

Buy crack. That was my only direction. At the police station in north London where they were running the investigation I met with John and the DI leading the team. The briefing was pretty straightforward – they knew crack was being served up in their area but they had no idea who was responsible. They needed to find out. So for my first ever undercover job the only instruction I was given was to 'buy crack'. There was no name, no number, no target, no place to start at all. It was purely a fishing expedition. When I strode out of the station and walked towards the main road an hour later, I was determined to come back with the goods. I was nervous as hell. It felt like there was so much at stake here. There were up to twenty other officers on this job with me – working as my safety team – and they were all relying on me to make it happen. The sheer weight of expectation was huge but I tried not to think about it too hard. I'd come dressed for the job –skanky green anorak, battered tracksuit bottoms and scuffed-up trainers. I had my hair pulled back tight in a ponytail and I'd rubbed some baby oil through the roots to give it an oily sheen. I'd smeared mascara around my eyes for that 'up all night' panda-eyed look and chewed Black Jacks to give my teeth a grey, dingy colour.

Come on, Dan, I thought as I loitered on a busy main road before sitting down at the bus stop to take stock. I had to find a place to start, I had to find someone to 'nut' into. I watched people coming and going. The Budgens grocery store was busy with customers and a homeless man was sat at the entrance, begging for change. He might know someone but there was very little way for me to engage him without it looking totally obvious. On the other side of the road I noticed a bookies – a couple of people stood outside, smoking. They definitely appeared more promising – if anyone looked like they might use crack it was the guy on the left with the long, yellow fingernails and rake-thin frame. I headed inside, greeted by the sound of the racing results from the TV sets on the walls, while half a dozen men sat on stools and tables in a room that stunk of stale smoke and detergent. A couple of punters glanced over in my direction as I slid onto a stool next to the guy I had just seen smoking outside.

He was filling in a betting slip but he seemed to be having trouble locating something, rummaging through his coat and jeans.

'I wrote it on one of these . . .' he muttered, fishing out betting slips from the pockets of his coat. He seemed on edge – perhaps he was rattling, needing his fix. Crumpled pieces of paper piled up on the counter. I picked a couple up and started examining them.

'Whatcha looking for, mate?'

'I got a tip. Now I can't fucking find it. Lingfield, today. Three thirty . . .'

'I'll look for you.'

I searched among the scraps on the table in front of him. Eventually we found the piece of paper he was looking for and he placed his bet.

We got chatting and I told him I was in the area visiting my nan. This was my 'legend'. I figured that telling someone I was visiting my nan would be a pretty safe bet. It explained why I was in north London and out of my own area without inviting further questions. After all, who was going to know my nan? We talked about nothing for a while and then, after half an hour I asked if he knew anyone serving up. He didn't react at first, concentrating hard on the screens in front of us. His slips were spread out on the table – nothing big, just a few quid a time – all lined up one after another.

Shit, have I blown it? I didn't speak, waiting for him to answer.

'Who for?' he asked after about a minute's silence.

'My bloke.'

More silence.

'I'll take you if you chip me off,' he offered. *Bingo!* 'Chip me off' meant he'd help me score if I let him take, or 'chip', some crack rocks off for him. Technically, if I did it myself it could be considered supply of a class A, so I had to avoid that. I could always hand the rock back to the dealer to chip him off instead of doing it myself.

'Yeah, okay.' *Whatever it takes to make this work.*

'Right.' He carefully gathered up his slips into a pile and put them into his pocket. 'I ain't got another runner for a while. Let's go.' We walked out together.

On the street he checked up and down the road.

'There's our bus,' he said, nodding. 'Just a couple of stops up to Turnpike Lane.'

'Nah, I ain't getting on no bus wiv you,' I said.

'Why not?'

'Costs nothing to walk.'

'Yeah, all right,' he shrugged. What did he care? He was getting free crack. There was no way I could get on a bus to our destination – I needed to stay visible to the safety team from the Haringey drugs squad. They were all around me, on foot and in various vehicles stationed around the area. They needed to keep eyes on me the whole time and that couldn't happen if I was on a bus. I had a mobile phone in my pocket with an open mic so the team knew exactly what was going on. We set off on foot.

'Here, you want this?' he pulled a couple of gold chains from his pockets and handed them to me. One had a locket on and the other a gold cross. They looked like someone's personal jewellery.

'What's this?'

'Got them from a friend, he's asked me to sell 'em for him.'

'I don't need a necklace.' It was obvious they were both hot. I handed them back.

'I'll do you a nice deal – tenner for the pair.'

'Nah.'

'They're good. Look at the hallmarks! That locket alone is worth twenty. Seriously, that ain't shit. Altogether they're worth fifty quid, I reckon.'

'So sell 'em to someone else. I'm not interested.'

'A tenner. Come on.'

For a minute I wavered. Should I buy the jewellery? It was surely evidence if it was hot and could be worthwhile intelligence if the owners were identified. They could be someone's precious items, someone who would be very pleased to see them again. Also, in a strange way, I felt sorry for this guy. He looked like he could use a break and clearly believed we were in a position to help each other out, but I wasn't sure this would be a sensible diversion of my funds. Plus, I wasn't a hundred per cent certain about the legality of paying for stolen property.

We walked up the busy main road for a good half hour before turning off down a side road of terraced houses. The place was secluded and I knew it wouldn't be easy for the safety team to keep eyes on me in this spot. I just hoped my phone mic was working okay. We stopped by an ordinary-looking house on the road. It was typical for this area – not in great condition, with paint chipped from the window frames and net curtains. But nothing that would make you look twice. I handed over twenty quid before my fixer ordered me to wait at the front gate while he walked up the path and knocked at the door. It opened a crack to reveal a large man in his thirties. They started talking in whispers. Meanwhile, at the upstairs window, I spotted a curtain twitch and another guy looked down at us both, as if assessing me. He nodded once: *Yeah, all right.* Then the fella who'd opened the door handed over the crack. My fixer took his cut, gave me the rest and left.

I was ecstatic. My first undercover job and I'd made it work! I put the crack into the pocket of my anorak and turned to leave. Just then, the guy at the door said: 'I'll walk you.'

'Nah, that's all right. I'm good.' *I don't need this.* I was going to go back to the safety location and that would be it from me.

'I'm coming,' he insisted as he closed the door behind him and followed me back up the path.

'Where you heading?' he asked as I turned back onto the main street.

'To my man at my nan's house.'

He started walking with me and now I couldn't get him to leave. What did he want? How was I going to get rid of him? Surely he didn't want to come all the way back to 'my nan's'!

'Who's it for?' he asked.

'It's for my boyfriend. I've got to get back to him now. I've been gone ages. He's going to kill me if I don't get back soon.'

'Where is it?'

'I plugged it,' I said, meaning I'd shoved it up my arse. I hadn't, of course, but I was afraid he wanted to steal it back. *What does this fucker want?* The longer we walked, the more nervous I felt. Back on the main road I kept up a brisk trot as he strode by my side. Then, unexpectedly, he grabbed my arm and pulled me down a little alleyway by a pub on the corner. He had a firm grip and since he was about six foot and eighteen stone there was no way I could fight him. Now I *knew* what he wanted.

'Come on.' He pushed me up against the wall of the pub.

'No. Don't. Get off. I told you, I've got a man.' I tried to shove him off me as he fumbled for the zip on my jeans but he was strong.

'I'm pregnant!' I blurted out. 'Just . . . DON'T!'

I was desperate now. This guy was not giving up.

'No no, darling . . .' he murmured. 'You don't have to fuck me, you can just suck my dick.'

He leaned against me, pinning me against the wall, his hands moving from my trousers to his own.

'No, I can't. I can't. My boy'll kill me . . .' I felt like crying. I couldn't escape. If I tried to squirm away to run to the main road he'd easily outpace me and then he'd probably hurt me. The realization was sickening. *Shit, this is going to happen. This is really going to happen and there's nothing I can do to stop it.* He was undoing his trousers and started to pull me down towards his fly.

Oh god.

Oh no.

Just bite and run, Dan. Bite and run!

'YOU FUCKING SLAG!' a furious shout erupted down the alleyway.

A white van had pulled up at the entrance and a bloke had jumped out, someone I recognized from the briefing earlier in the day.

'Oh my god, it's my boyfriend!' I exclaimed. I'd never been so pleased to see another human being in my entire life.

'WHATCHA THINK YOU'RE DOING?' he bellowed, marching up the alleyway and grabbing me by the arm.

'Jake, don't! Jake! Nothing happened. I swear . . .'

'All right, all right mate . . .' The big guy let go of my arm. 'Calm down. Nothing happened.'

'DIDN'T I TELL YOU? DIDN'T I TELL YOU NOT TO FUCK ME AROUND?'

'Yeah, Jake. I know. I know. I know. You're right . . .'

He flung me into the back of the van and I pulled the door shut in a hurry. *Thank fuck for that!*

Back at the safety location, the team were thrilled. They were impressed that I'd managed to keep hold of the drugs considering what happened. I could very easily have given up the crack to save myself but, to be honest, that wasn't an option as far as I was concerned. I didn't for one minute consider going back empty-handed. I'd done what I set out to do and the reaction of the team was encouraging.

The detective inspector approached me. 'Well, Danielle, I thought I had big balls but yours are huge.'

I was flattered, though still a little shaky and scared. These were long-serving officers and it meant a lot to hear a compliment like that.

'You took your time,' I joked with 'Jake'. 'That guy was not taking no for an answer.'

'Yeah, I could tell, but you can handle yourself, right?' he said, a note of admiration in his voice. 'You're an Essex girl, aren't you?'

'Well, even Essex girls have standards,' I countered. I was never going to let on just how scared I'd been during the incident in the alley. It was only later, washing the baby oil out of my hair in the shower, that it hit me how close I had come to being assaulted. It really was a matter of seconds. If

'Jake' hadn't turned up when he did I was going to have to deal with that guy's dick. I shook my head. *No, best not to dwell.* This was by far the most exciting police work I had ever done and I wanted more.

I was deployed again very quickly and every time I was sent out, I came back with the goods. More success meant more jobs and that suited me just fine. I was hooked on the adrenalin and I loved it.

And so began my new double life as an undercover police officer. To my friends and family I was just an ordinary copper on the streets of London, coming home at night and weekends to enjoy the life of a good-time Essex girl. I had my nails done, took frequent sunbeds and spent two weeks every summer in Marbella. It was all blow-dries and nights in Mahiki and Chinawhite when I was off the clock. And with all the extra overtime for SCD10, I could afford to buy myself a few 'nice' pieces in the sales. I loved good clothes, beautiful handbags and designer shoes, splashing out on Burberry, Versace, Dior and Gucci. I even wore my super-comfy black Prada trainers when I was in uniform. The criminals loved it.

'Look at you in your Prada!' they'd marvel. 'Look, bruv! She's got Prada trainers on!'

'Yeah, yeah, Prada, that's right,' I grinned. 'You're nicked.'

But at night, when I was deployed to the streets in my undercover role, I was a whole different Danielle. I took off my nice nails, put on my skanky unwashed anorak and trackie bottoms, rubbed oil through my roots and I went off to buy drugs. In fact, I went back to the address off Turnpike Lane several more times after that first buy. The big guy never tried anything on after meeting Jake and he was happy enough to keep selling to me. It was standard practice to go back to a dealer several times to establish their pattern of behaviour so that the defence couldn't argue it was just a one-off. We needed to ensure they wouldn't wriggle out of a charge once it reached court.

I never told anyone what I was doing, not even my mum. I knew she'd only worry about me, as she had done every day since my heart problems as a child.

Things were going well between me and Tom, but I also felt no need to share with him the details of my UC work. I figured that if he didn't know, he wasn't obliged to keep my secret, and the last thing I needed was for it to accidentally slip out to the other officers in my borough. Tom and I often worked opposite shifts, so he wasn't aware when I was posted out of borough. As far as he was concerned, I was 'job pissed', taking overtime because I simply loved police work. And it was true to some extent – I was job pissed, but not by ordinary police work.

It started out around once a week. My phone would go and I'd hear the familiar Scottish voice: 'Danni, I've got a little job for you.' I could refuse if I wanted but I never did. I enjoyed it too much and fortunately my guvnor was great, letting me off all the time to work for SCD10. Although I was officially employed by the Met, I soon became a UK-wide asset, being deployed up and down the country, taking sometimes two or even three jobs a week. Quite often, I could work the UC deployment into my normal shift pattern, but at other times it would have to be overtime which, if I had less than five days' notice, was double pay.

At that time, British Transport Police (BTP) ran their own UC unit (which has since been disbanded). If they could produce evidence there was a drug supply within one mile of a railway line, they could take the job from the local police. And since they had no women on their team, they called on my services quite a lot. One of the first jobs I did for them was in Eastbourne in East Sussex. This sleepy retirement town on the south coast harboured a serious heroin problem and the BTP needed to identify the dealers who were serving up in the area. One day, a lead came in from a local informant – or snout, as we called them – and BTP called me down to establish the strength of the tip. It was just a telephone number, but that was a fairly common way into the supply line. Informants, usually heroin users, got decent money for good quality intelligence.

I took the train down on a Friday afternoon and was picked up from the station to meet the team. The plan was to try the number and if the dealer agreed to meet me I'd be deployed immediately to get the goods. It would have to be a speedy turnaround, so the rest of the safety team were sent out on standby. Meanwhile, I went into the toilets with my kitbag to change out of my own clothes and into my standard 'street' clothes. My kitbag had everything I needed for my undercover work – a couple of pairs of shoes, money, cigarettes, lighter, skanky coat, tracksuit bottoms, baby oil for the hair, mascara to rub around the eyes, make-up remover and a few Black Jacks. Not only did they give my teeth an unhealthy colour, but eating them while getting served up was a tactic I liked – if the dealer told you to 'mouth it' – put the drugs in your mouth to hide them – you could refuse because you were chewing.

Once everyone was in position, the detective sergeant, myself and another officer shut ourselves in an interview room with the tape recorder going and I called the number from a mobile they gave me.

One ring, two rings, three, four . . .

'All right?' a male voice answered.

'Yeah, I need to pick up.' I spoke with some urgency. 'Can I come get some?'

'Yeah yeah . . . I'll meet you outside McDonald's.'

'Right, how long?'

'Ten minutes.'

I looked at the DS and he gave me the thumbs up. I wasn't familiar with the area so I had no idea how long it would take us to get to McDonald's from the station, or whether they could get the rest of the team in position that quickly.

'Okay, but don't be long,' I urged. 'I need it now.'

'Yeah yeah yeah . . . see you in ten.'

And that was it. He hadn't asked me who I was or how I'd got his number. There were no nice introductions in this world. Generally, dealers didn't want to be on the phone any longer than they had to, and neither did I. Perhaps I had expected a little more enquiry from the dealer. In London, there might have been a smidge of suspicion, a question as to how I'd got the number. But this guy just didn't care.

I hung up and we all swung into action. The DS got on

the phone to the team, ensuring they were all in place, while the other officer showed me on a map where I needed to go. I pegged it out the back of the station, into the safety car and was dropped close to the high street. In a few minutes I was standing outside McDonald's looking as shifty as possible. I made eye contact with another guy, who was looking just as shifty as me. He nodded and a minute later a car pulled up.

'You waiting?' It was the same voice I'd heard on the phone. He was in his early twenties, dressed in an Adidas tracksuit and a navy cap.

'Yeah,' I said.

'What do you want?'

'Two and two,' I replied. Two white (crack) and two brown (heroin).

'Forty quid,' he said. I had the notes ready in my hand and gave them to him, he handed over the wraps and I had a very quick look before putting them in my coat.

'Okay, I'll ring you later . . .' I said and stood up.

'Yeah yeah . . .'

And then he was gone. I shuffled back the way I came, got in the safety car and returned to the station where I wrote my statement and clocked off. I was on the train home half an hour later. That was what I loved about doing UC work – I just flew in, did my bit and left. I didn't have anything to do with the investigation itself, I didn't need to file lots of paper-work or spend hours on background checks. I got the drugs, the adrenalin rush and the kudos. And once it was done, I went back to buy from them again and again, to prove that these people were established dealers. The dealers themselves were happy enough to keep serving me. They wanted money, after all.

I loved it, though it was ironic that I had grown up as a 'good girl', an upstanding and law-abiding citizen, careful not to incur so much as a speeding ticket or a parking fine my whole life, and had now embarked on a career buying class A drugs all over the country.

6

Girl for the Job

After around six months on the team, I was invited to my first social event with the UC crowd. We were just wrapping up a job in central London when the DS pulled me to one side.

'Hey, Danni. Fancy coming out for a drink tonight? A few of us will be down the Red Lion on Beak Street later.'

I gave him a casual 'yeah, all right' but inside I was dancing! It wasn't a big deal to them, of course, but to me, getting an invite to their weekly social was like being accepted into their gang – and they were the coolest gang I knew. I legged it back to Limehouse Police Station as I had a locker there with everything in – like Mary Poppins' bag! – changed out of my 'crack' clothes and spruced myself up for a night out. I have to admit I felt a bit nervous the first time I walked into the pub. I was still fairly new on the team, and I had only met a few of the other UCs by this point.

'Danni!' the DS called me over. His name was Vic and he was a short and mean-looking guy. In any other situation I would have been scared of him – he had a hard south London edge and I thought of him as the Bulldog. The other officer who ran our team was Michael. He was completely different – tall, big in every way and very corporate-looking. He always dressed smartly in suits, had short, neat hair trimmed to his collar and generally was a lot more 'polished' than the Bulldog. He reminded me of a boss in a mafia movie, always impeccably turned out but with a sinister edge. You knew you didn't want to get on the wrong side of him.

It turned out that Vic and Michael were the best of friends. That night I found out a bit about their backgrounds and how they'd found their way into UC work. In the last few years, they'd worked closely with international teams on some big cases, dealt with gun crime and a lot of high-profile law enforcement like the FBI. My jaw was on the floor as they regaled me with stories of the jobs they'd done together. They also introduced me to a few other officers. One or two I recognized from the course but several faces were new to me. I have to admit it was great to be able to talk freely with other people doing the same work. I could be the real me, for a change. It turned out this pub was their regular hangout spot. Nobody really met up in the SCD10 offices at Scotland Yard because of the risk of being seen by the press. If we were briefed it was usually at a secure address or the police station where we were conducting the investigation. It just wasn't smart to be seen coming and going from one of the most notorious build-ings in London, a place where there were usually a fair number of photographers and TV camera crews stationed.

In our unit we had around fifteen UC officers in total – from all different ranks across the force – and what I came to realize over time was that no two officers were the same. There simply wasn't a UC 'type'. We each had very different, individual profiles, strengths and approaches. There may have only been a handful of women but there was certainly no other Danni. For example, we had one chap who was really posh – he was an art fanatic and he could infiltrate high-end gangs who stole art to order. There was one guy who was absolutely disgusting to look at. He had long, straggly unwashed hair, wore clothes that were literally falling apart and grime seemed to be attached to every part of him. But he was one of the cleverest people I'd ever met and a highly successful officer. There was a guy who was fluent in Russian and sported Russian prison tattoos, a mixed-race girl who spoke Jamaican Patois which was very useful for certain deployments, and we even had a guvnor. He was very active and, surprisingly for his rank, he was deployed a lot. But he wasn't in charge of the unit – he had his own borough to run. Everyone had their own specialisms and their own strengths so that, whatever the situation, there was always one of us who could take on the deployment. And when it came to drugs, I became the girl for the job.

John was my handler. He was the one who called me with the jobs. But Michael ran the unit. If I had a problem with the scheduling, he would usually be able to sort it out with my department head in Tower Hamlets. Now I started going to the Red Lion on a regular basis, not because I wanted to drink particularly, but to get to know the team and pick up tips. Since the work was sporadic and spread out, we rarely met other UC officers unless we were deployed together. Besides, I was still earning my stripes on the street jobs and could use all the help I could get.

On a drizzly Saturday evening one October I found myself deployed to the unofficial red-light district in Barking to stand on the corner and catch kerb-crawlers. My first test was to 'pass' with the other girls – if they saw me as a threat or suspicious it could jeopardize the whole operation. I wore a pair of tight grey jeans, black faux leather jacket, heels and a low-cut top. Fortunately, none of the women gave me a second glance as I walked along the line, all of them spaced out at regular intervals down the main drag. Just the opposite, they were really friendly.

'Oh hiya, love,' a woman in a skin-tight red dress and denim jacket greeted me warmly as I stopped next to her. She had dark roots peeking through her blonde mane and looked around forty years old. 'Haven't seen you for ages, darling.'

She thinks she knows me! I didn't know whether to feel offended or flattered.

'Nah, I've been down south for a bit,' I said, scanning the street. 'How's it tonight?'

'Busy. Word of warning – Ginny said she spotted a CID car earlier, blue Ford Focus. Two blokes.'

'Yeah? Cheers for that. I'll keep an eye out.'

Just like with buying drugs, I had to be careful with the way I spoke to the punters. The main issue was not to act as an 'agent provocateur'. Dad had told me to look up this term before I took the TP course in Hendon – his only advice, as it turned out. At the time I thought it was just an underwear label! In fact, it was a fundamental concept of UC work and it had been drummed into me that we weren't allowed

to act as an agent provocateur, which meant enticing somebody to do something they wouldn't ordinarily do. When I
was posing as a 'working girl', for example, I couldn't offer
anyone my services. I had to wait for the bloke to proposition
me. So when a car stopped to pick me up, I would lean in
and ask the driver: 'Yeah? What do you want?'

'Are you working, love?'

'What do you want?' I'd say again, a note of impatience
in my voice. I couldn't confirm that I was soliciting so I just
repeated my question. Then the guy would often come
straight out with his request and I'd wrinkle my nose in
disgust and say: 'No! I'm waiting for a cab. Eurgh!'

These cars were then followed by the CID team and picked
up round the corner, once they were well out of sight.

The requests were usually pretty standard – hand jobs,
blow jobs, straight-up sex – but occasionally you'd be asked
for something really weird. One time a guy called me over.

'Yeah, what do you want?' I asked.

'Dry anal,' he replied. *Jesus. What did that even mean?*

That put the level of banter up a notch back at the office!
Catching kerb-crawlers all night was a long shift, but quite
often an arrest would morph into something more. Some of
the drivers we stopped turned out to be drink driving or had
drugs on them. The worst was when one guy approached me
with his kid in the back seat. That was horrible. Another
time a guy pulled up with his dog in the car and snarled at
me, angrily: 'I just want to fuck you hard.'

He was aggressive and intimidating. I was glad when they
picked him up. The officers back at the nick weren't quite as

thrilled, as they had to find something to do with his dog! Sometimes we were out there because the working girls had reported an abusive or violent punter and we were specifically looking for a suspect to bring in for questioning.

There was nothing glamorous about this kind of work – it was long, tiring and full of the worst examples of humanity. So it was a real step up the day I was asked to do an escort job at a fancy hotel in central London. This time, instead of making myself grubby, I had to glam up. *Finally!* I thought to myself as I headed into town with a budget for my 'escort' wardrobe. I always preferred to source my clothes myself rather than have someone else choose my outfits. For this job, I picked out a French Connection dress, Gucci heels and some classy jewellery. I topped this off with a beige wool coat and one of my own handbags. Truth be told, I was a bit of a bag freak and had a growing collection of designer handbags in the spare bedroom of my little flat. This one was a classic leather Gucci GG print with bamboo handles – one of my favourites.

As usual, the brief wasn't too specific. Somebody was serving up to the escorts and I had to find out who. I walked in the front door, nodding at the top-hatted doorman, and turned into the swanky bar and restaurant area. *Wow – now this is a bit different from hanging around grubby backstreets buying crack.* There was a wall of enormous mirrors behind the long bar at the back of the room, low comfy chairs decked out in expensive designer print and rows of upholstered benches along the extravagantly wallpapered walls on the other side. The whole place felt rich and moneyed – it even smelled rich, owing to the floral scent of an enormous vase of lilies arranged elegantly on the centrepiece table. I felt giddy for a minute. *Where do I even start?* Tables were filled with twenty-some-things enjoying after-work drinks, couples on dates and small groups of 'creative' types in funky clothing. Until this moment, I had no idea the place was also brimming with escorts, either looking for work or waiting for punters. To my untrained eye, they just blended into the crowd; well-dressed women waiting for a friend at the bar or sitting at low tables on their own. I needed to suss it all out. I spotted a good-looking woman on her own at the bar, sipping a glass of champagne. She looked very glamorous with honey and caramel highlights, a gorgeous handbag, great nails and an air of pure sophistication. Now this woman looked interesting . . .

I hopped onto the barstool next to her and ordered a glass of champagne. The bartender opened up a page of the bar menu to show me a whole list available by the glass. I had no idea what to choose so I just said: 'House is fine.'

The woman was scrolling through her phone. *Here goes nothing . . .*

'I love your bag,' I started. I did actually. It was Fendi – one of my favourite brands.

'Got it in the sales,' she said. 'Harrods.'

'The Harrods sales are the best,' I smiled. 'I go every year. Bought a Versace jacket in January marked down from two grand to four hundred.'

'I've got the most exquisite little red Versace dress I've been wearing forever,' her eyes sparkled. 'Literally, forever. I think I'll be buried in it.'

I laughed and that was it. I was in. She introduced herself

as Lily and we started chatting about our favourite designers and all the secret sample sales we'd discovered. After twenty minutes her phone buzzed.

'Wait here a sec,' she said. 'I've just got to run outside.'

The front of the bar was glass so when she went out I could see everything. A sleek black car had pulled up to the front entrance and she leaned in to do something . . . It looked to me like there was a little transaction going on. A punter or a dealer? I couldn't tell. When she sashayed back – in what I now knew were Louboutin heels and a Dior dress – she ordered us both another glass of champagne.

'What is it?' I asked, nodding to the guy outside.

'Oh, I just picked up something for the night.'

'Oh, who are you getting it from at the minute, cos it's really dry round here, isn't it?

'I'll give you his number,' she offered. Brilliant! She was as good as her word and I sat there for a couple more hours, chatting with my new friend. I couldn't ring the number straight away as I didn't have permission and the calls needed to be recorded for evidence. *Well, this isn't bad*, I thought to myself. *It certainly makes a change from freezing my arse off all night on the streets.* Eventually, Lily's phone buzzed again.

'Okay, this is me,' she said. 'I'll see you around.'

I have to admit, I enjoyed hanging out in that hotel. I felt like Billie Piper in *Secret Diary of a Call Girl*. I went back the following week and though I didn't see Lily again, I called the number she'd passed on and was served up by her dealer. I returned around twice a month after that and met a few more escorts as well as a couple more dealers, part of the same gang, who sold me coke, or what we called 'gear'. They were a Turkish outfit, we discovered, a well-oiled machine servicing the higher-end clientele of the drugs market. Whenever I called, they rolled up in nice cars and charged £60 for a gram of cocaine, instead of the usual street price of £50. The stuff was no different, of course, they were just adding a service charge for delivering to a nice hotel. When we had enough evidence, we got a surveillance team on them, then they were rounded up and arrested for possession with intent to supply, as well as a number of other offences, since they were a part of a major organized crime group. By the time they appeared in court, the evidence was so over-whelming they had no choice but to plead guilty.

It wasn't just on the street or in classy hotels – I also bought drugs in nightclubs. For one job in Leeds, me and Nic were deployed as a team. It was the first time we'd been put on a job together and it was good to spend some time catching up as we travelled up on the train. Nic's covert deployments were different from mine. She would buy weed or pills. She would also do decoy jobs, but she ran her own team within CID so couldn't be deployed as regularly. Nic isn't a girly girl at all so she wasn't up for the 'dresses and heels' jobs. When we got to Leeds, we were briefed by the DI leading the team with what was now a familiar line: someone was serving up, they needed to find out who. That night Nic and I donned our clubbing gear and headed out to score. I was wearing a tiny purple dress with ruffles that was actually sold as a top, so it was arse-skimming short. Nic wore camouflage cargo pants and a T-shirt.

As we walked through the security barriers and found our way through the dark corridor to the entrance hatch, we were hit by the loudest thumping techno I'd ever heard in my life. Nic and I looked at each other – it was pounding, unrelenting trance. Hmmm . . . not my cup of tea. We got drinks, headed to the dance floor and danced for a bit, checking the place out before moving to the courtyard in the back. It was a good excuse to get chatting to people while they smoked. Actually I hated smoking, but I taught myself how to do it for my UC work because I could see it was a good way to nut in.

''Scuse me, mate, you got a light?' I asked a chap in the courtyard who looked like he might be dishing out. He looked me up and down. *Cheeky fucker*, I thought. *He likes the look of my dress!*

'You're not from round here,' he observed. *Genius.*

'No, I'm not,' I giggled, turning on the girly, flirtatious charm.

'Where you from?'

'Essex.'

'I like Essex girls,' he grinned wolfishly. *Yeah, I bet you do.*

We chatted and smoked while he admired the dress. There was obviously an advantage to being a feminine woman in certain situations and I wasn't above using my charm to get what I wanted. Men like this guy also held assumptions about Essex girls and that played to my benefit too. In his eyes, I was too dumb to be a cop.

'You don't know where I can get anything, do you?' I asked.

'What you after?'

'What you got?' I didn't want to ask for anything specific for fear of limiting what I could get. If he had it, I'd take it.

'Who says it's me?' he teased.

'You said you could get it.'

'Yeah, but who says it's me?' This guy was playing very hard to get but I was never one to give up easily.

'I'm not saying it is you but what you got?'

'I've got pills, do you like pills?'

'Yeah, I love pills. You need them on a night like this, right?'

He pulled out a little bag from his jeans and looked at me with a mischievous smile.

'I'm going to shell these pills in your mouth like I'm shelling peanuts. Open wide!'

Then he started flicking pills towards me. I looked at Nic. *Shit, what the hell do I do now? I can't catch them in my mouth. I need to take them back for evidence.* So I dived off in the opposite direction to the pills, pretending to miss them every time, gathering them up with my hands and putting them straight into my handbag.

In the early hours we left the club and went back to the station to write our notes. The pills went to the lab overnight for testing and the next day, a Saturday, the results came back positive so we returned to the club to find our guy.

'Can you get anything else?' I asked.

'Yeah. What do you want?'

'Great, let me take your number.'

From this point on we went up to Leeds every other

weekend, where me and Nic bought MDMA, coke, ecstasy and ketamine off this same guy. It was a pretty successful job and once they had enough evidence the team swooped in and our part was done.

A few months later, I was at a pool party in Marbella on a girls' holiday with Three Bellies and the Arse when we got chatting to a group of men. We quizzed them on where they were all from and they answered variously east London, Birmingham and Leeds. My ears pricked up when I heard the last guy say Leeds.

'Oh, I love Leeds,' I enthused, recalling my weekend trips. 'What do you do there?"

'I own a nightclub.'

What? My heart started to pound.

'Nice, what club is it?'

'Well, actually, it's just been shut down cos we had under-cover Old Bill in there buying drugs.'

'Noooo!' I feigned shock. 'That's terrible. I'm so sorry.'

My stomach did a little flip and I turned back to the girls for a second.

'We are not police,' I mouthed.

My heart was beating at a million miles per hour and I felt quite panicky and breathless. What are the chances? Would he recognize me? I'd spent hours in this guy's club . . .

'And what about you?' he asked. 'What do you do?'

'Me? I'm a florist.'

7

This Wasn't the Plan

'Woah! What is that?' I exclaimed when I was presented with an enormous motorhome at Cumbria police HQ. I had just been briefed on my latest UC job where myself and Rich, a male officer, would be buying ecstasy pills. Over the last few years there had been a spate of drug deaths at summer music festivals and the local force were nervous about their upcoming event. Theirs was the biggest festival in Cumbria, it brought a lot of tourism to the area and they weren't keen on attracting bad publicity. So we were here for insurance. I was about to attend my first ever music festival.

'That's your home for the next four nights,' said the DI. 'A top of the range Winnebago – shower, bed, kitchenette, toilet. It's got everything.'

'I've got to drive this thing? It's a truck!'

'It's a very *expensive* truck, Danielle, so please, treat it nicely.'

Me and Rich hopped up into the cab of the Winnebago and after a cursory introduction to the controls, I started the engine and with great care manoeuvred the huge vehicle out of the car park and onto the road. After a little bit of time, I got used to the length and weight of the vehicle and before long we arrived at the entrance to the festival site. It was a murky, overcast afternoon as we were given our wristbands, all-access passes and directed to the plot for the campervans and motorhomes. This was a long gig – four days – so I knew we had to pace ourselves. First things first, we needed to change into our dancing gear and orientate ourselves. I wiggled into my hot pants, zipped up my neon hoodie and pulled on my newly purchased wellington boots. I even went so far as to apply a little glitter on my cheekbones and shoulders. *Well, when in Rome!* Rich laughed when he saw my navy Hunter wellingtons.

'They're a dead giveaway . . .' he smirked. 'Far too posh for a festival.'

'If I have to encase my feet in ugly rubber boots, darling, they're not going to be cheap shit like yours,' I shot back. I loved my Hunters and wouldn't hear a word against them!

We had a little walk around to get our bearings, making a mental note of where everything was situated: the tent field, the main stage with the bands (which was already muddy and gross), the dance tent, food area and toilets. There were a number of other officers in plain clothes dotted about who would be our safety team for this event, as well as a fair number of uniformed police for general security. The most noticeable thing was that everyone here was so young. *They're all kids*, I thought to myself. There was nobody older than about twenty-two. I felt like I was back in school!

Later that night we hit the dance tent, which was noisy and dark and full of kids gurning their faces off. *This is where we'll score.* It was dark in the tent but everyone was wearing sunglasses, including myself. I danced for a while, pretending to be off my face like everyone else, before clocking a bloke standing on the edge of the dance floor. I nodded at him and he nodded back. There was no need for any conversation – he wouldn't have been able to hear much anyway over the trippy house blasting through the speakers.

'What you after?'

'What you got?'

'I've got Molly, Es, ket.'

'I'll have two pills.' Rich had danced his way over.

'Do you want?' I asked him, piggy-backing him into the supply.

'Yeah, what you got?'

'Pills.'

'I'll take two.'

This was great. So now we had two buys from one person. The guy gave me the pills, I handed over the money. There was no suspicion on his part, no attempt to even hide what he was doing. It was as easy as a trip to Boots! The best thing, I realized, was that I didn't even have to account for my east London accent. This was a festival – everyone here was from all over the country.

The safety team in the tent saw the deal and waited until the bloke went to the toilets to arrest him. Meanwhile, we returned to our Winnebago where we handed the pills to the officers waiting to take them to the lab, quickly wrote up our reports and then went back out to buy more drugs. We did this five times that first night until there were no more safety teams in place to make arrests. Then we sat on the steps of our Winnebago and unwound with a beer each. I was surprised at how easy it had been. Nobody was suspicious, nobody asked if we were Old Bill. It didn't feel as if there were organized gangs operating here, just opportunistic, small-time dealers out for a good time. Most were off their faces themselves! It was easy pickings, there was no skill to it and, to be honest, I enjoyed the job. I danced, listened to some good music and soaked up the happy, party vibes. The only hardship was sleeping in the damn Winnebago.

We worked the dance tent again on the second night and this time, one lad had run out of pills so he offered to walk us back to his tent to get some more. As soon as we had done the deal, the team moved in and swept up his whole tent. Most of the dealers pleaded guilty to the charges but this one guy fought his case. He was a law student in his second year at university and four months after the festival I was back up in Cumbria to present my evidence in his court case.

'Which one is he?' I asked our counsel as we waited to go through to the courtroom.

'There he is,' the barrister pointed to a young lad in an oversized suit, probably no more than nineteen, who looked for all the world like a child. He was sandwiched between an older man and a worried-looking woman in a corduroy skirt and navy quilted jacket, obviously his parents. The three of them looked totally out of place here. For the first time I felt uneasy about the prosecution. *God, we're charging him with possession with intent to supply. It's a really big offence – this could ruin his future.*

Sitting there, waiting to present my evidence, I was hit by

a wave of guilt. Was he a drug dealer? I suppose technically yes . . . but not really. He was just a young boy who would have gone on to a good career if he hadn't taken a chance at the festival and got caught. It could have been someone else – it could have been some people I knew. The risky choice he made, combined with a bit of bad luck, ruined his life. It bothered me, this case, and for months and years afterwards my mind kept returning to that image of a barely grown boy in court, over and over again. Was this the best way of dealing with drugs? Maybe the risks could have been dealt with in other ways, like testing the drugs on site to keep people using safer. This method has become more popular in recent years and I believe it is now the standard way to maintain drug safety at music festivals in other countries. I wish it had been around earlier, and here in the UK, to be honest. You're not going to stop drugs at a festival with a couple of undercover coppers buying from five people. All you need to do is ensure the people taking the drugs are safe and know exactly what's in them.

It wasn't long after the festival that I missed a period. A fleeting thought crossed my mind, which I quickly dismissed. Nah, I couldn't be pregnant! I was still with Tom but we were careful and always used protection. It must have been the funny hours I was keeping. I reckoned it had thrown my cycle out of whack. Back in London, I was deployed to Tottenham to nut into a gang of lads selling heroin. The first deal had been easy – too easy, as it turned out. They sold me mud.

'Little fuckers!' I fumed when the results came back.

'What do you want to do?' the DI asked.

'I want to kick the shit out of them, that's what,' I snapped. I felt embarrassed.

'When?'

'Today!'

Those shits, thinking they can chin me off. How dare they? I raged silently as I strode towards the little green where this group of lads hung out, psyching myself up for a confrontation. In fact, it was fairly common to be sold crap if you were new to an area. Dealers often took the piss if they thought they could get away with it. They may never see you again. More money for them. But I was furious they had dared to try it on with me. As I approached the group sitting on a bench, I saw the guy who had sold me the mud two days earlier, chatting to two others.

'YOU FUCKING MUGGED ME OFF, YOU CUNT!' I exploded, throwing the cling-film wrap of mud at his face. 'MY BOY SLAPPED ME BECAUSE OF YOU, YOU FUCKING PRICK! I WANT MY FUCKING MONEY BACK.'

'Woah woah woah,' he jumped up, palms in the air, shocked at the ferocity of my attack.

He was around six foot tall. And that was just him – his mates were big too. Still, I wasn't backing down now.

'YOU FUCKING ARSEHOLE!' I ranted. 'DON'T THINK YOU CAN TAKE ME FOR A FUCKING MUG! HOW DARE YOU! CHINNING ME OFF. I TOOK A BEATING COS OF YOU.'

I kept on at him and his eyes darted left and right, alarmed at the scene I was causing, right in front of a busy tube station. He didn't need this drama.

'Look, come with me. Come with me,' he urged and I followed him round the corner to a walled area. He served me up again. I examined it closely this time – it did *look* different to the brown nugget he'd given me before but for all I knew it could be mud again. I had a hunch, though, that he wasn't going to try to rip me off a second time.

'What about the other day?' I said. 'I want more than that, because you mugged me off and I've taken a fucking slap for you.'

He gave me some more gear and I left, shaking. I don't know what happened to me during that confrontation but I was totally immersed in my character. I felt no fear, no worry about my personal safety. If I was really buying gear for an addicted boyfriend and I'd just spent his last tenner on mud there was no way I would let this guy get away with it. Now I could go back and buy gear again and he knew not to mug me off. I was pleased that I'd gone back to fix the supply. It wouldn't have looked good to my command if I'd accepted the first deal and slunk off with my tail between my legs.

Two days later, I did a pregnancy test and it came back positive.

'What do you want to do?' Tom said when I told him. I knew what he meant.

'I'm not thinking of an abortion, if that's what you mean,' I said quietly. 'But, I don't know. I mean, it's not a good time, is it?'

'Erm . . .' Tom rubbed his chin. 'I'm . . . well, it's up to you, isn't it? I'll support you. I mean, whatever you choose, and if you want to have the baby that's great. We'll tell work . . .'

'Wait!' This was too much too soon. 'I can't think straight right now. Give me a bit of time, okay?'

'Okay, but you can't stay on frontline duties, Dan. It's just not right.'

'I know, I know. Just let me do this my way.'

For some reason it took me a long time to process the news that I was expecting a baby. At first, I buried my head in the sand, losing myself in work. I was twenty-one and my career was going so well. Tom and I had only been dating for a year – this really wasn't the plan. What about my dad? He'd be so disappointed in me. I just couldn't think about it, so put it to the back of my mind for a while and carried on. It was easy enough; I didn't get sick and I didn't change shape in any way. I was still tiny for weeks, fitting easily into all my clothes. In the end it wasn't the risks I took as an undercover officer that forced me to face reality, but an incident that took place as part of my borough duties in Tower Hamlets.

I was at the tail end of a night shift with Mick when we tried to pull over a car being driven erratically.

'Looks like a drink driver,' Mick nodded. He was driving tonight while I was the operator. I checked the clock: 5.32 a.m. We were a little under half an hour from the end of our shift. This was known as the 'fishing hour' for cops on the beat, because if you worked half an hour over the shift end you wouldn't have to come in the next day.

'Yeah, he's all over the place,' I agreed. 'Let's stop him.'

Our blue lights flashed, the siren blared but the driver didn't show any signs of slowing down or pulling over. On the contrary, he sped away from us.

'Uh-oh – he's running,' Mick murmured. 'Right, let's stay with him.'

So now we 'followed closely', which in police parlance meant we were chasing without actually admitting that we were chasing. Only advanced police drivers could officially pursue, so we were obliged to remain at 30 miles per hour. Which we did. Just.

We called it into the borough as well as putting out a call on the pan-London radio set to report that we were in pursuit. This radio was transmitted to all the London boroughs, so if we crossed into another borough they could take up the pursuit. Mick was an amazing driver and he kept up with the vehicle as it swerved, changed lanes and veered down back roads. All of a sudden, the car took a sharp right and we followed, right into the path of an oncoming bus. It was heading straight for us. *Fuck!* I braced for impact but Mick put his foot down and the bus missed us by a few feet. Meanwhile, the car we were chasing smashed into the back of a parked black cab and we screeched to a stop behind it.

The driver got out and started running. Mick and I both jumped out the car at the same time. I checked inside the crashed vehicle to see two women in the back seat of the car. Their legs had been crushed by the force of impact, concertinaing the back seat into the seats in front, and neither could move. They were trapped and crying in pain but neither were in any immediate danger, so we called for an ambulance and started running after the driver while I gave commentary on my personal radio. Mick was bigger and fitter than me so he got to the guy first and when I turned a corner they were on the ground, fighting. Then I heard the most blood-curdling scream I've ever heard.

'BASTARD BIT MY ARM!' yelled Mick. 'He bit my fucking arm.'

Mick's arm poured with blood, I tried to rack my asp – it's supposed to extend when you flick it – but the thing just wouldn't rack. *Fuck. Mick is losing this fight. The guy is going to kill him.*

Other units were on their way but right now I knew I had to do something. I grabbed my personal radio and smashed it over the guy's head. Hard. The radio split, his head split. Blood spurted out from his forehead but this nutter was still going, still beating on Mick. *Do something. Do something.* I kicked the bastard in the face. And still he kept going, pummelling away at Mick. I pulled my leg back a second time and swung again with all my force, this time smashing my boot right into his mouth, knocking out a load of his teeth. His head reared up and he fell backwards off Mick.

Now the other units started to arrive and several coppers jumped on the guy. We had actually crossed over into Hackney so they were all from another borough.

'You are under arrest,' I snarled as they put the cuffs on him. 'For assaulting a police officer. And that's just for starters!'

We might have been in another borough but this was my arrest – it was *always* my arrest. I made sure of that. We nicked him and took him back to the station where he had to see the doctor first before we could book him in. I had actually picked the guy's teeth up and handed them back to him before sending him off to the cells. *Well, he might need them back at some point.* It turned out he was high on crack, which was why he was chomping on Mick's arm. The two women in the car were prostitutes he had just picked up and after the fire brigade got them out they were taken to hospital where they found one had a broken pelvis and the other a broken leg. Poor women had got in the wrong car that night! We added GBH to the charge sheet.

After we locked him in the cells, I did a few searches on the guy and found that not only was the car stolen but that he was wanted for a number of other offences. I added the charges to the sheet and went to visit him in the cells: 'Just so you know, you're being further arrested for the offence of burglary, possession of a stolen vehicle and failing to stop . . .'

In the end we charged him with seventeen offences. By the time I was done I'd stayed around four hours past my shift end. Mick was in hospital, pretty beat up, but thankfully he had no serious injuries. I visited the office where the officers were due to carry out the interviews and I could see from the looks being exchanged between them they weren't happy. They knew they would probably spend the whole day interviewing this guy. I didn't care. I walked out the station that day high as a kite! It had been the most amazing arrest and we were the talk of the station. My elation didn't last long.

I woke that afternoon to a terse text from Tom: We need to talk.

When he came round that evening he was less than impressed. He'd heard all about our dramatic arrest the night before, as well as the near miss with the bus and the three-way fight.

'This is ridiculous, Dan,' he berated me. 'You're pregnant! You should not be on the streets kicking the teeth out of six-foot crackheads. Something could have happened to you or our baby.'

'Yeah, you're right,' I said.

'Of course I'm right. You can't keep taking risks. How would you feel if you'd got hurt tonight and lost the baby? How do you think I would feel? You can't carry on like this. You've got to tell work.'

'I will,' I agreed. It was time to face the music. I'd spent too long hiding from the truth but Tom was dead right. It was irresponsible to keep putting myself in harm's way. And as much as I dreaded the thought of being confined to a boring desk job, I knew I had no choice.

'Tomorrow. You need to tell them tomorrow,' he insisted.

'I will. I will, Tom. It's just . . .'

'What?'

'I've got to tell my dad first.'

8

Undercover Mother

The next day, as Tom drove me into work, I plucked up the courage to call my dad.

'Dad, it's me,' I started. 'I've got something to tell you – are you sitting down?'

'Well, I'm sat on the edge of the bath, Danielle, tiling the bathroom. What is it?'

'No, sit down properly.'

There was a pause. He realized I was serious.

'I'm not going to like this, am I?' he said.

'No. I'm pregnant.'

For a second, I held my breath.

'I'll ring you back,' he said. And he hung up.

I was devastated. My career had been going so well until now. He was the only one who really knew what I was doing and it made him so proud. But there was no way I could go back to covert work until I'd had the baby. I covered my face with my hands and stayed like that for a couple of minutes.

'He'll be all right,' Tom tried to reassure me.

'I know . . . it's just . . . I just feel shit. That's all.'

Worse was to come. As soon as I got into work I went to

speak to the inspector. When I told him that I was expecting, the first thing he asked was whether I had told my dad. I nodded sadly. I guess he could tell this wasn't planned because I didn't appear to be brimming over with excitement at the prospect of having a child. There was a genuine sense of puzzlement in his voice when he said: 'Okay, we'll have to take you off frontline duties. So tell me – where do you want to go?'

I never had any interest in office-based police work but I ended up in the Borough Intelligence Bureau and, as a compromise, the inspector let me work shifts instead of clocking in nine to five Monday to Friday, which would have killed me. As it turned out, the intelligence bureau was a good gig. There were five of us in the office, including two people I got on really well with – a male colleague who was approaching retirement and my friend who had transitioned from male to female. I have to admit – I really enjoyed it. The five of us got on well and had a laugh together, running our little hub, providing intelligence to my old response team. It was our job to look up any intelligence the teams needed while they were out and brief the next shift taking over. We were like personal intelligence officers for the teams on the ground and I liked to stay one step ahead. If I recognized any names or addresses of the calls going out, I'd do a quick background check and brief the officers responding.

'Mick, just so you know, that address is known for firearms.'

Just a little heads up could make a big difference to the

officers carrying out the searches and it satisfied the part of my brain that enjoyed spotting patterns and making connections.

It was a whole lot better than going into duties and sorting out the rotas, but it didn't match the thrill of actually going out myself on a night shift. Nights were always great in Tower Hamlets – there was always so much going on, no two night shifts were ever the same. *This is just until the baby's born*, I told myself. *Then you go back to work properly.* I was determined to pick up where I'd left off. The same was true for my undercover work. Even though I could no longer go out on UC jobs, I kept my hand in with the team by offering to 'stooge' for them on the TP courses. This meant role-playing different characters during the training, putting pressure on the trainees to see how they'd react. I discovered that being on the other side of this equation was a lot more fun! I learned from speaking to all the other UC officers on the course that the challenges weren't designed to trip people up exactly, more to bring out their strengths and test their ability to think on their feet.

As we emphasized to the trainees, the most important aspect to all covert work was working out a viable 'legend' that could withstand enquiry without arousing suspicion. Many failed this basic test. We heard plenty of people claiming to be users themselves, for example. You could kill that legend stone dead in one sentence: 'Come on then, we'll go and do it together and I'll give you yours for free.'

No genuine user would turn down free crack, so if the officer said 'no' it would look highly suspicious. When I was working out my own legends, I spent hours thinking about what to say and how best to protect myself. Saying I was in the area to visit my nan was helpful because it meant I had a good excuse for not being local and prevented further enquiries about my personal life. But I still needed a little knowledge of the geography when I was buying somewhere new. After all, it wouldn't be the first time visiting my 'nan', so I did a little digging. I might use the police intelligence systems to see what had happened recently and then I could drop a few references into the conversation, so it would seem that I was in the know. I noticed that a number of the women on the courses employed legends claiming to be working girls. As soon as I heard that my heart sank. *You're gone*, I thought. It made no sense for them to say they were a prostitute, because then they'd likely trade sexual favours to get a fix, and coppers can't offer sexual favours for crack.

If I couldn't do real UC work, helping out on the training courses was the next best thing and I enjoyed staying in touch with all the UC officers I'd got to know in the last few months. I felt it was important to demonstrate that I wasn't going to disappear just because I was pregnant, and they were pleased to have another woman on the team. I helped out on some of the more advanced courses too. The next one up was called the NUTAC course – National Undercover Training Assessment Centre – and it was designed to prepare officers for deeper and more dangerous covert work. For these jobs, the UCs went further undercover, sometimes being given whole new lives in order to immerse themselves fully into a group. We'd take the most promising UCs out to see how they'd behave in a real environment and show them the residence where they could be living. They weren't all particularly nice places – quite often they were dirty, small and dingy – but the right sort of set up for their new identity. Personally, I wouldn't want to live in the majority of them, but these officers were about to go long-term undercover so they had to acclimatize to their new environments.

They weren't just buying drugs, either. In one scenario I was paired with a male trainer while the officer taking the course was tasked with trying to buy a gun from us. Many of these scenarios were played out in real places rather than at the training locations and for this 'deal' we met in a large supermarket car park. I was in the driver's seat of a silver Vauxhall when our trainee approached the car.

'All right?' I said, looking him up and down.

'Yeah, I'm here to pick my thing up,' he said in a low voice.

'I don't know what you're talking about,' I replied. I wasn't going to make this easy for him.

'You know, the *thing* my mate talked to you about. The piece.'

'Get in the car.' I motioned for him to get into the back and he opened the car door and climbed in. Big mistake! He should have known better than to get into the car with us but I guess he was desperate or he forgot the rules. He repeated what he'd said about his mate setting up the deal to buy the gun and my partner in the passenger seat pulled out a replica from the glove compartment and pointed it at his face: 'What – this gun?'

'That gun . . .' said the officer, slowly. His whole body tensed up and his eyes darted to the doors, checking the exits.

'What are you nervous for?' I asked.

'I'm not. I'm not nervous.'

'Yes, you are. Are you a copper?'

'No.'

'You are. You're a fucking copper.'

'I'm not!'

'Take your clothes off,' I instructed. 'Go on. Take your fucking shirt off. NOW!'

The guy scrambled to get his shirt over his head to prove he wasn't wearing a wire.

'And the trousers!' I ordered. So he undid his jeans and wiggled out of them, sitting there in just a pair of boxer shorts.

'GET OUT THE FUCKING CAR!' I yelled. 'YOU'RE OLD BILL. GET OUT!'

So now the guy, completely nonplussed, climbed out of the car in his pants and shoes and stood there as we drove off with all his clothes still in the car! We found out later he was stopped by supermarket security, who wondered what a half-naked man was doing in their car park. We debriefed when he got back (and we'd given him his clothes) and told him what he'd done wrong. Actually, that guy passed the course and we did lots of jobs together afterwards. He was a really good undercover officer but in the moment we went with our instincts. None of it was planned. He had made one mistake in getting in the car and that's why we'd stripped him. But it wasn't about his mistake, it was about watching how he dealt with the situation as it developed and how he handled the pressure. He didn't buckle – that was the important thing.

I'd always wondered how they decided which of the trainees would stay and which would be sent home and found out pretty quickly that there wasn't a 'score' on each trainee. It was all much more informal. At the end of each day the tutors got together for a bit of a scrum, asking each other: 'What do you think of so and so?' Generally, most of us shared the same opinion as to whether somebody was good or not, though in all honesty mine was probably skewed because I was so happy to be part of this world. There were times I thought someone wasn't too bad but then I'd listen to the others criticizing them and I'd go along with the majority opinion. I was more likely to give a trainee the benefit of the doubt whereas more experienced officers were unwilling to take a chance on someone they felt was a risk. On other occasions it was pretty clear to all of us when someone wasn't cut out for this kind of work.

Dad had called me back, of course, the day I'd told him I was pregnant. Even though he admitted he was disappointed with the timing, he said he was happy for me if this was what I wanted. We talked everything through. Both he and my stepmum – and my mum and stepdad – were very supportive and agreed to help out with the baby when I went back to work. I was lucky – the pregnancy was easy and straightforward. Apart from a little sickness at the start, I felt fine and my bump was so small and neat you would never know I was pregnant if you looked at me from behind. Tom, meanwhile, was still living in his house-share until about a month before the birth, at which point we agreed it would be sensible if he moved into my flat. Dad was concerned when he heard about our new living arrangement.

'That's your flat, Danielle,' he said. 'Don't you think you better get something in writing? Protect yourself.'

'I don't know what you mean, Dad. He's not going to make off with my flat. We're having a baby together. Where else is he going to live?'

To my mind we were building a future together so I had no qualms about Tom moving in. On the contrary, I didn't want to be on my own when our baby was born.

Two weeks before I gave birth, Tom went down on one knee with a Tiffany box in his hand.

'Oh my god, Tom!' I whispered, thrilled to see he'd been shopping at every Essex girl's favourite jewellery store.

'Danielle, you are about to become the mother of my child. Would you also do me the honour of being my wife?'

I said yes. Of course I said yes! I mean, admittedly, I needed a microscope to find the tiny diamond attached to the ring and I wasn't all that certain Tom and I were a hundred per cent compatible, but then I had a great career, we were expecting a child together, and I just assumed that marriage came next. And to be absolutely honest, I was a little scared of doing this alone.

Tom introduced me to his parents and it was a shock to find out just how different our backgrounds were. The first time we pulled up the driveway towards a grand manor house to meet his dad and stepmum I assumed we were looking at a collection of individual apartments.

'So, which one do they live in?' I asked.

'What do you mean – which one?'

'Which apartment is theirs?'

'All of it – this is their house.'

'All of it? Seriously? Tom, your family are really rich!'

I'd grown up on an estate; Tom's family owned an estate! And while me and my siblings had all fought it out at the local comps, Tom and his siblings had attended private schools and were now off pursuing impressive careers in finance, IT and law.

It was like being introduced to a whole new world. The first time I saw them hanging their birds, fresh from a 'weekend shoot', I was shocked.

'What's that?' I pointed at the dead animals.

'A brace of partridge and three pheasants.'

'What are they hanging up for?'

'You hang game birds for flavour.'

'Oh right, not to scare off visitors, then?'

The family were all pleasant enough but I felt way out of my depth, like Alice through the looking glass. Tom's parents had divorced many years earlier so I met his father in Hertfordshire while his mother's home was up north, in Liverpool. On my first visit to his father's place I was asked if I ate fish.

'Yeah, sure,' I replied. I'd been brought up on cockles, whelks and rollmops so I assumed I was well set up for whatever they had in store. But at dinner they set down three huge langoustines on my plate and I had no idea how to eat them. I sat there for a moment in polite silence, watching everyone else, and then copied the way they cracked the head off and peeled the shell from the body.

Tom had mostly grown up in Liverpool so he had a lot of his friends there and he went back on weekends when he had four days off in a row. I went up with him too and met his mother but, as the pregnancy progressed, I wasn't too keen on spending hours sitting in the car. About a week before my due date, when Tom was in Liverpool, I had a 'show'. I rang my mum, who accompanied me to Basildon Hospital in Essex. They confirmed that the 'show' was a sign of the early stage of labour but it would take some time before I was in active labour and, in the meantime, I could go home.

Two days later, I went into labour on my due date but I didn't give birth until thirty-three hours later. It was a marathon, and a pretty terrible one at that. Tom wasn't the most helpful birthing partner. He kept crunching loudly on Hula Hoops, which drove me mad because I hate the sound of chewing. It sets my teeth on edge. But when our little girl arrived I fell instantly in love – she was small, cute, squishy and hairy, the most beautiful, perfect human being I'd ever seen in my life. Amelia arrived 8 pounds 3 ounces and hungry! But I was so tiny that I didn't produce enough milk to satisfy her. She was waking up all the time and no matter how long I fed her it only held her for a couple of hours and, since it was always me during the night because of the breastfeeding, I never got enough rest to replenish my supply. One morning Tom found us both asleep, hanging off the end of the bed. It terrified me. What if I'd dropped her and hurt her? That scared me into giving her a bottle and finally we both slept properly.

I tried to enjoy these early weeks with Amelia but if truth be told, I felt lonely and isolated. I was still so young and none of my friends had children yet so there was nobody to talk to during the day. At 9 a.m. I'd take Amelia to the creche at the gym while I had a workout and after that I'd wonder: 'What now?' There were no 'mother and baby' groups to join, no social media to link me to other new mums in the area. I was alone. As much as I loved Amelia, it was hard to fill the hours. So why stay at home, bored out of my mind, I reasoned, when there were jobs just waiting for me to do back at work? After twelve weeks I went back to policing and both Mum and Dad were brilliant with childcare. It was a wrench to leave Amelia for so long but I was determined that motherhood wouldn't derail my career.

Now my new home life revolved around taking care of Amelia. It felt as if the majority of the care fell on my shoulders, and Tom would still disappear to Liverpool for days on end. At first, I wasn't all that bothered. I had both sets of grand-parents – my mum and stepdad and my dad and stepmum – who all adored Amelia, and I assumed things would get easier with time.

Meanwhile, it was full steam ahead with our wedding plans. We had found a lovely country manor up in the Peak District and planned the big day for summer 2005. I had an image in my mind of how things could be between me and Tom and I hoped that we could make things work.

9

Falling Apart

'Cheers!' I raised my champagne glass in the air and Harry, my dining partner, mirrored my movements.

'To you, my darling. My beautiful princess!' he toasted.

'To me!' I giggled and threw back the rest of the bubbly till there wasn't a drop left in my glass.

'More!' I said.

'Yes, indeed,' he said and raised a hand to stop a passing waitress. 'We'll have another bottle of the vintage Veuve Clicquot.'

'My absolute favourite!' I gave a little drunken applause to the wine glass.

If only I had half as much fun at home as I did at work, I thought wryly. But there was no time to dissect the troubles in my personal life right now, I had to focus on the job in hand. There had been rumours about this restaurant in Mayfair for a few years, but recently the central London team had received intelligence pointing towards a money-laundering operation. So I was deployed with Harry, another young UC, to suss things out. Tonight we were posing as a wealthy young couple out for a good time and, after buying an eye-wateringly expensive meal and splashing the cash on vintage champagne, we'd received a couple of brandies on the house from the owner. Our flashy antics had caught his attention.

'You are a gentleman,' Harry drawled, raising his glass in the owner's direction. 'Come and join us, please.'

Harry pulled the chair out for the owner – a small bald man in a grey three-piece suit. Harry was privately educated and had that particular confidence that seemed to be instilled into people whose parents paid a fortune for their schooling. It was a swagger, a sense of belonging that you just couldn't imitate. Nothing fazed him, nothing impressed him. He was comfortable in almost any environment and tonight he was sprawled out on his chair like a king at a medieval banquet.

'You two look like you're enjoying yourselves,' the owner smiled indulgently. 'I like to see people having a good time in my restaurant.'

'You have a first-class establishment here, my good man,' Harry nodded approvingly. 'I was just telling my fiancé Danielle that we must hold the rehearsal dinner here. I can't imagine a better venue, frankly. Can you, darling?'

'No, it's perfect. We've got sixty for dinner in September.'

'Sixty-four now. Tim and Tabby are flying in from LA and the Goldsmiths have also confirmed.'

'Sixty-four . . . And there might be more.'

'Do you do private hires?' Harry asked.

'We do everything here, sir,' said the owner with an impish grin. 'Everything.'

The three of us sat drinking and chatting for a while, knocking back champagne and brandy. I was already woozy before the spirits arrived but now I knew I was getting properly drunk. *Shit, better keep it together*, I thought, as a waiter refilled my glass. Harry may have been a strapping six-footer but I was tiny. Thank god we'd eaten at least!

'You two want to come to my club?' the owner said eventually. 'It's a private members' club. Very exclusive. You are welcome as my guests this evening.'

'Sure,' said Harry. 'Why not? Let's make this a night to remember.'

So after we'd settled our bill we followed the owner through the back of the restaurant and down some steps where we entered a dark, low-lit corridor. A woman in a tight black tuxedo waved us through the double doors and we found ourselves in a dark lounge with plush velvet sofas and small tables set up with candles.

'Follow me.' The owner walked straight through the lounge, past a cocktail bar towards a narrow, curving corridor and into a back room which was clearly his office. It was like something out of *Scarface*! Scantily clad women draped themselves over leather Chesterfields while thick-set men in badly fitting suits played pool and smoked. At each end of an enormous mahogany desk in the middle of the room sat little mounds of white powder.

'Help yourself!' said our host. 'It's the best gear in town. Please. Take!'

Harry and I looked at each other – we'd hit the jackpot! *Shit, he's so drunk he is actually swaying*. Harry may have been big but we'd drunk a lot already and now I could see he was a little nonplussed as to what to do next. Somehow we had to get this stuff back to the lab for evidential purposes.

'Thanks,' I said to the owner, opening my handbag, placing it under the corner of the table and, using a credit card, scraped a large portion of the white powder into my bag.

'What are you doing?' the owner asked.

'Taking it, just like you said.'

'In your bag?'

'I'm a lady,' I explained daintily. 'I won't do it in front of you.'

'Oh, I see. Well, we can have someone bring it to you if you like.'

Harry raised an amused eyebrow in my direction – he thought this was quite an ingenious way round our little dilemma. We stayed a couple of hours in that sordid little back room as we chatted with the owner while some of his 'couriers' came and went. This was the beating heart of their coke empire and we'd wormed our way in on our first encounter.

Admittedly, Harry was an impressive UC. He certainly knew how to finagle his way around. He told our host he was in private equity and, if he found the right partner, he might be interested in investing in a new club. That really got our guy salivating. Eventually we wrapped it up at around 3 a.m. and Harry and I staggered out and walked round the corner to the safety location where we met the car to take us back to the station, but Harry had brought his bicycle and was determined to cycle back to Charing Cross. He got as far as the end of the street, wobbled and fell off, so he ended up being driven back too. All in all it had been a very successful operation and we got some great intelligence, but my god, we were drunk by the end of it all! I scrawled out my notes with one eye half-closed and got a cab home. When I woke up the next morning I had the worst hangover in the world. It had been a fun night and I was pleased with our results but we had winged it, making stuff up as we went along. Our legends really weren't solid enough to justify being in that position.

Tom still didn't know anything about my undercover work and I had no reason to tell him. By now I had sold my flat and we had bought a three-bedroom house in Wickford in both our names. To the outside world my life looked perfect – good job, nice house, new husband, beautiful daughter – but you didn't have to scratch far beneath the surface to see that things weren't as wonderful as they looked. Tom and I didn't make each other happy. One evening – during dinner with his mum and some other members of his family – things just came to a head and I realized I'd had enough.

I looked him straight in the eye: 'I want a divorce.'

'So do I,' he retorted.

The thought of divorce had crossed my mind before then but I always dismissed it. I felt that Amelia's needs came first, and it was more important for her to have her mum and dad with her. But I couldn't do it any more.

I pushed my chair back from the table, thanked his mother for dinner, got Amelia from her cot and drove back to Essex alone. Eventually he came home and we agreed to put it behind us. But the friction just seemed to grow and grow.

Things went downhill pretty rapidly with Tom because not long afterwards he found my covert work phone. I was out on a run when he went through my UC kitbag and made the discovery. There were messages on there from various people I had been in touch with for my UC work and, stupidly, I had failed to put a lock on it. When I got home he was standing in the hallway, holding the phone. Understandably, he thought the worst.

'It's not what you think.' I said. 'It's a work phone. I've been doing covert work for ages. I haven't told you because I couldn't but now, well, I suppose I have to.'

I sat him down and explained everything, but he didn't believe me.

'I'm not having a bloody affair! If I tell you I'm going up to a festival it's not for fun, that's work. All those nights out with the girls, the weekends away. It's work. So yes, I have been lying to you and I'm sorry but it's not to have a shitty affair. It's my job.'

He looked away and for a second I could see he was trying to match up this explanation with the things I'd said to him in the past. Then he wanted to know if my mum could confirm it. A fair enough question, but my heart sank.

'No, I haven't told her.'

No matter what I said he refused to believe I was a covert officer. Perhaps I should have told him earlier. Perhaps I should have trusted Tom with the truth rather than let him find out this way. But it was too late now. The trust between us was shot and it became clear that we couldn't get it back. *This has got to stop. We've got a child together.* We had one last trip to France to try and fix things but it was too late, there was nothing left between us and when we returned I told him it was over.

'That's fine,' he said. 'But I'm not leaving the house. You want it to be over? You leave.'

So I left. I took Amelia, still only three, and left with just a couple of bags of clothes, staying with family until I found a flat to rent in Chingford.

It was the most stressful time in my life. My mum, dad and stepparents all helped out loads but it was still a difficult period. In the end, I didn't care about the money, or the house or anything else. I just wanted things to be calm for Amelia's sake. I knew from my own childhood just how awkward things could be for children of warring parents and I was desperate to smooth things over. One weekend Tom took Amelia up to Liverpool to see his mum and instead of bringing her back to me the following Monday as we had arranged, he didn't show up. He had his reasons, of course, but it drove me mad. That day I went to see the inspector and explained that I had to take a day off work to get Amelia.

'No, sorry. You can't take tomorrow off,' he replied.

'But he's got my daughter.'

'Is she at risk of harm?'

'Sorry, sir, but we're not dealing with a case. This is *my* daughter. He needs to bring her back.'

That was a shock. I had expected the management team at Tower Hamlets to be more supportive, but it appeared they had Tom's back rather than mine. *I can't work here any more,* I realized. *Not only do I constantly run the risk of bumping into him but they seem to be taking his side.* So I started looking for a job in another borough.

My life was imploding and now the stress really began to

take its toll. I took every UC job I was offered to earn enough money to support myself and Amelia, but also because it got me out of the borough and away from Tom. It was my way of escaping, if only for a few hours. I could lose myself in this other life, the fake life of an undercover officer, and pretend for a short while that none of it was happening. But I'd go home at night, consumed with guilt and misery. I'd put Amelia down to sleep, having barely seen her all day, and was overcome with shame. 'I'm sorry, I'm so sorry,' I whispered to her as she slept. 'Mummy's screwed up big time.' I felt so bad when I was with her. I'd wanted to give her a happy, stable home life, I wanted to give her everything she deserved, but I couldn't and that made me feel guilty all the time.

I started to fixate on losing weight. In the press at the time there was this all this talk about Posh Spice being a size zero and I decided that I should do that, I should get down to a size zero. Don't ask me why – my head was so messed-up. Perhaps it was a way of punishing myself, perhaps it felt like the only thing I could control at the time, but I basically stopped eating anything except vegetables and drank copious amounts of black tea. I took myself off for long, arduous runs and started abusing laxatives. Tom and I fought all the time about everything – the house, childcare, arrangements. I was so angry all the time, so frustrated.

One night, Mum came round to babysit – her and my stepdad were at my place all the time – and she looked pained when I took off my jumper to reveal my bony arms and shoulders.

'Your head looks too big for your body,' she said, appalled. 'You've lost too much weight, Danielle. There's nothing left of you.'

That didn't register. Nothing did. She told me over and over again I had to start eating properly, to look after myself so that I could be a good mum to Amelia. And I knew she was right in the back of my mind but by now I couldn't stop. I was taking a packet of laxatives a day and I'd become terrified of eating anything that might cause me to put on weight. Finally, she showed up one day with a picture of a prolapsed rectum brought on by laxative abuse.

'There!' she held it up to my face. 'That's what's going to happen to you if you don't stop this.'

That frightened the hell out of me, enough to start eating again. I felt a surge of optimism when I landed a new job at Chingford station, just up the road from my new house. *Maybe things are finally settling down*, I thought. Maybe we can finally start building our new lives together and put all the pain and struggle behind us.

10

Moving On

'Danielle, it's John,' the familiar Scottish drawl came on the line. 'I've got a little job for you. It's a pub in south London. We think a gang's running an operation out of there but we need intel so we want to get you in and run it until we've got enough to set up surveillance. Probably two days a week for a couple of months. What do you think?'

A pub job? This was a step up from my normal duties out on the street or in the hotel. This was a long-term infiltration project, the kind of job I'd been keen to try for some time.

'I'm definitely interested, John,' I said. 'I want to do it but I'll need to get it past Heather first. She's not been very cooperative the last few weeks, as you know.'

'Okay, well, talk to her, and if you have any issues just let me know and we'll get it sorted from this end.'

'Thanks, John.'

'Aye, no worries. Come by Abbey Wood station on Tuesday morning and we'll brief you there.'

It had been a huge relief when I landed the job in the Misper (Missing Persons) unit at Chingford Police Station in the borough of Waltham Forest. Of course I was sad to leave Tower Hamlets after so many years – I'd cut my teeth there,

I'd made good friends and I felt I knew every inch of that borough – but I needed a fresh start, a place where I could get away from Tom. Chingford station was just at the end of my road so I could drop Amelia into nursery each morning and then leg it to work, which was a hell of a lot better than commuting. There was even a primary school close by which would make things easy when Amelia turned four. The Misper job suited my skills down the ground. It was proper investigative work and I enjoyed hanging out with the two old boys in my unit because they let me take all the really interesting cases. These coppers didn't want to get out and about, talking to the friends and family of the missing person. They were there to finish off their police careers at a quiet desk.

Many of the people who regularly went missing became familiar to me over time, like vulnerable adults with dementia or looked-after kids who ran away from care homes. These were the easy cases, the ones we usually found within a day or two. Other cases proved much harder to solve and I would spend weeks trying to piece together the last movements of men or women who'd gone missing for no good reason. One eighteen-year-old lad had been reported missing by his family after a night out and despite extensive enquiries we were left scratching our heads with no leads at all. It really bugged me. There were no sightings, no CCTV captures, no eyewitness accounts, nothing. He literally disappeared in a puff of smoke. Then, two weeks later, the river police dragged a body out of the Thames and the post-mortem confirmed it was our boy. At the inquest the coroner had no choice but to record an open verdict because there was just no clue as to what had happened. Did he fall? Did he jump? Was he pushed? My heart broke for his family, not knowing how their beloved son and brother had met his final moments and why. I wanted to give them answers but, after putting in hours of research and investigation, we still had nothing concrete and I felt I'd let them down.

On the whole, the work was fulfilling, the location worked well since it was near to my new flat and my covert career was going strong. The only spanner in the works was my new DS, Heather Fisher. In the beginning, Heather had been happy to authorize my UC jobs, enjoying the prestige that a UC officer brought to her team. But when she realized how frequently I'd be gone she started to clamp down. After all, she'd advertised my job as a full-time position and with the hours I kept I was probably on a part-time schedule. On the last few occasions I had asked to be excused for covert work she had refused.

'I'm sorry, Danielle,' she said sternly when I asked permission to take up the new deployment. 'It's just too much time out of the unit. We need you here.'

'Okay,' I replied sweetly. I couldn't fight her on this. I didn't have the authority. So I called John instead and put him in the picture.

'For fuck's sake,' he growled, exasperated. 'She hasn't got a fucking clue! These jobs cost thousands to run and she's saying no for a Misper? Don't worry. I'll get Vic to sort this.'

Sure enough, Vic the Bulldog spoke to her and by the end of the day Heather had given me permission to start my new covert job in Abbey Wood. Technically, he outranked her, so she didn't have much choice in the matter and I think that pissed her off even more.

This is so fucking dodgy, I thought as I crossed the empty footbridge from the station and headed through the estate which housed the Queen's Head at the end of an ugly cul de sac. I'd dressed in my normal clothes – jeans, Converse and a nice top – nothing revealing or overtly sexual. I wasn't playing a particular role here – I had to present myself as close to the real Danni as possible to ensure I came across as authentic and real. After the briefing, I had taken the train to the station nearest the pub. I couldn't risk getting a lift in a car. This was an area nobody would go to unless they had a reason to be there. There was no passing traffic, a car could be easily spotted and identified as Old Bill. *I just hope I don't get mugged before I get there.* None of the safety vehicles were close enough to help if I was. Five minutes later, I turned a corner and saw a battered old sign hanging over a dingy pub. I pushed open the heavy wooden door and as I walked in I felt all eyes turn towards me.

'All right? Can I use your loo?' I asked urgently. 'I'm bursting.'

'It's round the back,' said the surly landlord.

'Cheers.'

I walked quickly through the small bar area to the ladies' loo. When I got there, I locked the cubicle door and sat on the toilet. *Breathe, Danni. Just breathe. You're going to be fine.* I gave myself a couple of minutes before coming out again, all breezy smiles.

'God, that's a bit better. Can I get a vodka and tonic?' I said to the landlord. As he was preparing my drink, I looked around. There were just three customers in the place. One guy at the bar and two more at a table in the corner. It was pretty nasty; sticky floor, dusty portraits on the walls, the kind of pub addicts visited to sell stolen meat and razors.

'Can I get you that?' the guy at the bar offered. He looked a little older than me and was smartly dressed in a pale blue button-up shirt, navy jeans and brown Gucci loafers. His auburn hair was trimmed neatly to his ears and he was wearing a good watch. The kind of watch that probably cost a couple of grand.

'Thanks,' I smiled. He pulled out a massive wad of notes and peeled one off for the barman. *Flashy. I think you're just my type.*

'I've not seen you in here before,' he said.

'Nah, I've come to see my nan. She's moved in up the road.'

'Yeah? Where you from then?

'Dagenham. I'm Danni.'

'Patrick. Well, Pat to my friends.'

'Nice to meet you, Pat,' I said, lifting the glass in his direction. 'Your health!'

And that was it. We started chatting. Pat seemed like a nice fellow and he took a bit of a shine to me, buying me several drinks over the next few hours as we chatted about all things under the sun: football, karaoke, our favourite bars in Majorca. We were so engrossed, in fact, that I missed all the calls on my 'dirty' (covert) phone. The next thing, I turned round and there was another UC, a detective sergeant, standing at the bar. Just standing there. He nodded in my direction. I checked my phone – *Shit, I've missed six calls.* I looked at the time – I'd been in the pub over five hours.

'Oh god, is that the time?' I exclaimed. 'Pat, I've got to go. My nan's making tea.'

'Listen, give me your number and I'll text you.'

I was in. At the debrief afterwards I apologized to my command but told them I had established a good connection with Patrick, who was likely part of the gang operating there. He had my number now and started to text me on my dirty phone, asking when I was coming back to the Queen's Head.

'I know you can handle yourself, Danni,' said the DI running the investigation. 'But just watch it with this guy. They're not a nice bunch.'

'Will do, sir.'

After that first encounter I went to the pub at least once a week, usually on a Friday when I was visiting my 'nan'. Pat was always there to meet me, spruced up in a freshly pressed shirt and wearing unbearable quantities of designer aftershave. Gradually, he started to introduce me to his 'buddies', the other guys who hung around the pub. They usually showed up in top-of-the-range cars and sat together on the same table in the corner. Once we were sitting together, the fellas spoke quite freely in front of me, none of them showing any reservation about me or my trustworthiness. It was amazing – I overheard some fantastic intelligence on their operations and by god, they were into everything. Robberies, drugs, guns – you name it. I just sat there, knocking back vodkas, soaking it all up. They spoke about their drug 'drop-offs', an armed robbery on a particular jewellery shop, robbing a van and several other jobs. They all wore designer clothes, had lots of cash and ran several phones each. Weirdly, I grew quite fond of them all, which is strange seeing as I was gathering evidence on their criminal activities. I think most people have a nice side to them and I find it easy to relate to people in general. But with this group I felt that their circumstances had led them into a world of criminality – it was what they were brought up with as a lifestyle. None seemed like they were out to prove anything, they were just normal blokes who were trying to get by the way they knew how. It might sound strange, given the circumstances, but I didn't really see any of them as bad people as such. And they made it so easy for me!

There was no question that it was a big advantage being a young woman in this situation. Sure, I played the 'dumb' card but I didn't have to work too hard. I was leaning into their sexist assumptions that a young woman couldn't possibly be a copper. And she definitely wouldn't have the brass neck to try to infiltrate their big boys' gang! The 'girly girl' act certainly helped and Pat was so keen it was sad. Each week he turned up with something new for me – flowers, gifts, handbags. I think that's a big problem for a lot of young, heterosexual men – if they think there is even a remote possibility that you like them, you have the advantage. The moment you make them feel good about themselves all rational thought flies out the window. A little touch on the arm here, some flirtatious eye contact there, and it's all over! It's definitely a weakness and one I exploited to the full.

Admittedly, it was a tough tightrope to walk. I'd created a certain expectation from my admirer but I had to keep him at bay. The odd pat on the arse I could cope with but one night he followed me to the ladies' toilets.

'Come on, Danni.' He squeezed up against me in the corridor and leaned in for a kiss.

I turned my face to the side and pushed him away.

'No! Pat. Stop it, will ya? I don't do that.'

'Ah, Danni . . .' His hands were everywhere.

'No! Look, come on. Just . . . just don't. I'm not one of them girls.' I pushed back hard this time and said firmly: 'I don't know you that well. Be a bit more respectful. I'm not kissing you in front of everybody.'

He stepped back, clearly stung by my rejection, but I could see he didn't regret having a try. And he would try again, I knew that. It was problematic, like a 'hurry up and wait' scenario.

But I persisted because the intelligence was just so good. One day I sat down at a table and the head of the gang, a tall bloke named Pete, was flicking through a copy of *AutoTrader* magazine. They were picking a car for their next job.

'Here, Danni, what one do you think?' he asked, spinning the magazine in my direction. *This is great! It's going to make things so much easier for our surveillance teams.*

'I don't like that,' I said, turning my nose up at their choice. 'It's boring. I like this one!'

I pointed to a purple Nissan.

'Fuck me!' Pete laughed. 'It's a hairdresser's car.'

'It's funky,' I retorted playfully. Pete was actually a good-looking fella, much better looking than Pat. He liked me too, I could tell. *Give me a bit of time and I can get into him*, I thought.

'You really want this one?' he looked at the car's spec.

'What?' I asked innocently. 'I think it looks great.'

'No, you're right, Danni. It's a decent car. Let's see what we can do.' And he stood up, took his phone outside and called the dealer. They were always outside on their phones, these lads. They were busy guys, into everything and most of them were pretty decent with me. Just one guy took the piss. I hated him. He was a classic slob and I didn't like the way he tried to bolster his own insecurity by smacking my arse whenever I passed. In the real world I would have made him pay for that, but since he was a part of the gang I had to bite my tongue for this job and that was frustrating.

After two months the boss took me off the job. It had all got too much with Pat and he'd started contacting me all times of the day and night. The DI was worried for my safety. Besides, they had reams of intelligence and the surveillance teams had collected plenty of evidence too. Not long afterwards they were all arrested during a cocaine drop-off and convicted of a number of crimes, including armed robbery, possession of an illegal firearm, handling stolen goods and possession with intent to supply. I was pleased, of course, but in the back of my mind I felt sorry for Pat. He had been the weak link in that group, the nice guy. The others were all hard men and if it hadn't been for Pat I wouldn't have got a foot in the door. They were told they'd been subject to a police operation but they didn't know it was me until the day I turned up in court to give my evidence. It wasn't always essential to give evidence in court, as quite often the intelligence we had gathered was so strong that the defendant pleaded guilty, but in this case Pete and two others pleaded not guilty.

So I went in, gave my first name (not my surname) and confirmed I was a serving officer. Then I was asked if I recognized any of the men in court. When I said yes, Pete shot me a nasty look. He seemed so pissed off to see me there. Immediately, we broke for recess and then I was told I didn't need to give any further evidence as the defendants had changed their pleas to guilty!

I felt pretty good about my first long-term infiltration job. It had worked out beautifully, though I saw in myself that I was never satisfied. I always felt I could get more. If Pat hadn't been so keen on me I might have stayed longer and got more intel, but that was the problem with going under-cover. There was always more intel you could collect, more evidence to gather, more crimes to uncover. I wanted to keep going but I didn't have a choice. At the end of the day it was the DI who called the shots, decided when the deployment was over. And looking back, it was probably the right call. Pat had become a nuisance. If we hadn't shut it down he might have gone further than making a few late-night calls. There were times he was texting when I was looking after Amelia. Some women might have found that disturbing but I didn't worry about him tracking me down at home – social media wasn't anywhere near as big at the time and there were no clues to lead him to my address. But I knew that every time I walked into that pub I took a risk. This was dangerous work and not everyone had the appetite for it. It was just as well I did.

What I didn't have the stomach for was conflict in my private life. I tried to be as accommodating as possible. I tried to ensure Tom had regular contact with our daughter and that Amelia's life was not disrupted. But the wrangling went on and one day I got a letter that broke my heart. He was suing me for full custody.

I tried everything to avoid going to court but things broke down during mediation so we had no choice, finally ending up in Holborn Family Court.

Frankly, I was embarrassed to be there. Nobody goes to family court through choice. In my professional life I'd worked with social services and the courts on some terrible cases where children were removed from their families – and for good reason. We were *not* one of those families. I chose to represent myself. I'd been to court plenty of times to give evidence so I had no qualms about speaking in court. I felt strongly that I hadn't done anything wrong and wanted to state my case to the judge. Nevertheless, it was a scary day.

I brought my dad along as my McKenzie friend, which meant he could be there for moral support without contributing to the proceedings or giving legal advice. But I have never been more nervous in my entire life – and that includes both my real life and my fake life. As much as I felt confident that Tom's application would be rejected, there was so much more at stake. My fitness as a parent was about to be put on the stand and examined in court. It felt like the courts had been invited to step inside my home, my private world, and judge it all. I found it so intrusive and stressful. I just wanted it all to be over so we could move on with our lives. It seemed Tom's main complaint was my objection to letting Amelia stay over with him during the week. This was purely a practical consideration. By now Amelia was in school and I felt it was unfair and disruptive – Tom lived an hour's drive from her school. Much better that he have her on the weekends or during his days off. I was trying to be fair to all of us and that included our daughter.

He came with his solicitor and we sat on opposite sides of the bench while the judge spent a little time explaining proceedings before putting Tom in the witness box. This was his moment – he outlined all his grievances against me. He wasn't happy with Amelia's school – which was the best in the borough – he claimed that I was being unreasonable, that he should play a part in school drop-offs and pick-ups and he felt I was unsympathetic to his concerns. But what surprised me most was when he brought up my undercover work, revealing to the court that my job involved buying drugs and posing as a prostitute. It came completely out of the blue and hardly seemed relevant! My dad threw his arms in the air in a manner that said: *What the fuck!*

'Mr Brooke – please, no gesturing,' the judge admonished.

'Sir, if I can explain?' I said. I really had to sort this out. He nodded.

'It's true I buy drugs as part of my job as a covert police officer. In that role I am also deployed in red-light areas to catch kerb-crawlers. I do not prostitute myself and I buy drugs solely for evidential purposes in the deployment of my police duties. Besides which, none of that has any relevance to anything we are talking about today.'

'I see. Thank you,' the judge said.

After Tom gave his evidence, it was my turn. I went in the box and put my case as clearly and succinctly as I could, arguing that I had never stopped Tom seeing his daughter and that my objection to the midweek overnight stays was purely to ensure she didn't have a long journey to school and back. Once it was over, we had to wait a few weeks for the judgement and when it finally arrived in a sealed document, I was relieved to see the judge had rejected Tom's request for sole custody, awarding us joint custody and putting in place sensible care arrangements. I felt quite cross about being dragged through the courts to achieve what we, as adults, should really have worked out for ourselves. Though at least now it was set and there was no arguing with the judge's decision. I was more than ready to put the drama behind us and move on.

11

When Things Go Wrong . . .

Once I'd demonstrated I was capable of pulling off long-term infiltration deployments, I was assigned more jobs of this kind, which I found rewarding. They were certainly more challenging than a straightforward drugs deal, with the potential to tap into a range of criminal activity. This meant building up my legend, working out the dynamics and relationships of the individuals involved and getting myself in with the right people. Things didn't always go according to plan. There were times I put in hours of legwork, building up intelligence, only for the job to be scuppered by something unexpected. That's certainly what happened in Beckton.

According to the DI running the investigation, they had noted significant supplies of coke coming from this one pub in Beckton and wanted to find out who was bringing it in and who was serving up. I was assigned to go in and suss things out. I felt confident from the start. It was an area I knew very well, since my aunt and uncle both lived there. For my legend I said I was staying with my nan temporarily after splitting from my boyfriend. This worked well for several reasons: being newly 'single' gave me an air of vulnerability and innocence. Since I'd recently come out of a big relationship I had the perfect excuse to keep unwelcome attention at bay. And of course my 'nan' was the perfect cover story for being in any area. They were unlikely to ask me who my nan was but if they did I was honest and told them it was Cathy. And that would be the end of that conversation.

On my first night at the pub I got chatting to the DJ – a guy called Dex who said he could get me some 'good gear'. He was sweet but a little suspicious at first. After all, I was a strange girl who had literally appeared out of nowhere.

'You're not a cop, are you?' he asked, half joking, half serious.

'Oooh, I would love to be a police lady!' I exclaimed, eyes wide with excitement. 'Can you imagine? That would be brilliant.'

'Are you serious?' said Dex. 'Who'd want to be a fucking pig?'

'I think it would be so exciting. I reckon I'd be good at it too.' It was a daring response but always seemed to work well. The implication, of course, was that I was far too stupid to realize why they were even asking me and therefore I couldn't possibly be Old Bill, so my inquisitor had no need to worry.

It was a question I came up against a lot in my work and I'd vary my answer, depending on who was asking and what situation I was in. Among some groups, it was better to act defensive and aggressive.

'Fuck off! Who you calling a copper?' I'd spit back, furious at the mere suggestion. Going on the front foot worked when you were dealing with gangs, since it was clearly a massive insult to call someone a cop. But there were days, like this one, it suited me to play dumb instead. My giggly, credulous response disarmed my accuser and allayed any concerns. Then, if I was asked directly what I did for a living, I kept it vague and untraceable, claiming to work for 'my family business in Essex'.

DJ Dex sold me coke a couple of times but I knew from the start that he wasn't the main dealer. After he handed over the gear I'd stay in the pub most of the night and watch him. He was getting it from someone else – a tall, good-looking lad who hung out at the back of the bar with two other blokes and a girl with long auburn hair. She must have been his girlfriend, because a couple of times I got chatting to him and she shot me murderous looks. But he was definitely the main supplier and I was convinced that, given enough time, I could get into him too.

On my fourth visit, I went to the pub for karaoke night and felt confident enough to wear a wire. I didn't normally wear a camera in the early days of a new deployment. It was an unnecessary risk if the target didn't know your face and might decide at any moment to pat you down. I'd been patted down a couple of times before and I knew from speaking to other UCs that wearing a wire too soon could be catastrophic. One officer had been subjected to a furious beating when his wire gave him away so I always had to feel very sure before agreeing to wear one. By now I had been in the pub on several occasions and my face was familiar. Once again, Dex served me up coke, though this time he got a bit cheeky and tried to follow me to the toilet. I didn't even realize until I walked into the stall and he walked right in after me.

'What are you doing? Get out!' I said, surprised to see him squashed up against the wall next to me.

'I'm going to toot with you,' he said.

'No you're not! I don't do that in front of men, no lady should do that in front of men, that's disgusting,'

'Oh, you're classy!' he grinned.

'Too right,' I said, finally pushing him out the cubicle. 'Now, leave!'

Having a gender-based modesty over snorting drugs was, admittedly, a bizarre reason not to 'toot' together but you'd be surprised how men accepted this without question. It really was quite easy to convince them that my refusal to do it in their presence was a question of manners!

By the time I went out again, Dex was safely back inside the DJ booth so I went to the bar.

'Hi – can I get you a drink?' it was *the* guy, the good-looking dealer.

'Yeah, that'd be great. Bacardi Breezer, please.'

'No worries,' he said and waved a note at the barman. I looked around for the long-haired girlfriend. There was no sign of her. So that was why he was approaching me tonight – she was away. He saw his chance and so did I! The only reason I hadn't been able to nut into this guy before was that she was always watching him. Tonight, however, it looked like I had a clear run at the goal. We started chatting and the longer we talked the more I knew that I could get some good intel on him. At some point he would ask for my number and then I'd be in.

Everything was going swimmingly until 10 p.m., when the

pub doors banged open and I heard a male voice shout: 'POLICE POLICE POLICE! STAY WHERE YOU ARE!'

Around thirty coppers in heavy riot gear stormed through the doors and at the same time, everyone threw their drugs in the air. It was like the whole place acted as one – customers, bar staff, the whole dodgy lot of them – and suddenly the air was thick with white powder. For a few seconds, time slowed down and I watched, mesmerized, as it seemed to be snowing indoors. Then chaos erupted all around me. I could not believe what was happening – people dived to the floor, officers grabbed punters, drinks came crashing to the ground and all of us were enveloped in a white, cokey mist. I heard a muffled yelp and looked over to see the landlord's dog take a leap out of the window.

'DON'T FUCKING MOVE!'

'STAY WHERE YOU ARE!'

'FREEZE!'

'POLICE!'

All around me the police were yelling in people's shocked faces and now I could tell from their shoulder numbers they were TSG – Territorial Support Group, the Met's public order policing unit. The riot squad, essentially. *Jesus Christ*, I thought as the pub erupted around me. *What the hell is happening?* One officer swiped his asp along the bottles on the side of the bar, smashing every single one. Glass went flying everywhere. This felt heavy-handed and unnecessary. There was no need for them to get so bolshy when it was clear that no one had any intention of fighting back. The only upside to the tumult was at least it had stopped the two drunk women at the karaoke machine murdering 'Dancing Queen'. But why on earth had thirty officers been sent into one pub . . . in riot gear?!

One by one, they grabbed each of us to be searched. My new friend, the suspected dealer, was searched and he had nothing. Most people had nothing on them because they'd thrown it away. The only person, in fact, who was holding that night was me, because I was hanging on to mine for evidence. The female officer who searched me looked like she'd won the lottery as she triumphantly pulled three wraps of coke from my back pocket.

'Oh, what's this then?' she asked in a self-satisfied tone.

I looked daggers at her, refusing to speak.

'You're under arrest for possession with intent to supply a class A drug,' she said to me. 'Cos that's a lot, isn't it? Three wraps. That's not just for you.'

The officer clearly thought she was a superstar. Technically, if someone has more than one wrap you can arrest them for possession with intent to supply – PWITS – a more serious crime than possession. What she didn't know was that of all the dodgy people in the pub this evening, the only person she'd managed to catch was an undercover cop.

I was taken outside, cuffed and sat on the steps on the back of the police van.

'You got anything else on you that you shouldn't have?' she asked, a very policey thing to say. I hated this woman right now. She'd ruined my job.

'No.'

'You're going to be strip-searched when you go back . . .'

'Yeah, I know.'

'So it's better for you if you tell us now.'

I shook my head in anger and disbelief. As much as I wanted to break cover, tell her what an idiot she was and demand to know how they could be so stupid as to bust a pub that was the subject of an undercover operation, I couldn't say a word. There was no way I could expose myself in front of everyone so I kept my mouth shut.

Eventually, I was loaded into the carrier and driven from Beckton to Barkingside Police Station, where I was taken into a room with the same female officer, who started strip-searching me. She didn't get far before she saw the camera attached to my top and stuck onto my chest, with the wire threading around my bra underwire. It took a couple of seconds for her to realize what had happened.

'Oh my god,' she whispered. We locked eyes. Now the enormity of her mistake hit her.

I said nothing. I had no idea who was in the cell next to me or who might be listening right now.

'Oh my god,' she said again and I rolled my eyes as I pulled myself away, buttoning up my clothes in furious silence. I just hoped she wasn't going to say anything monumentally stupid while we were within earshot of other prisoners.

'Okay, erm . . . back soon,' she said. *Thank god she hadn't blown my cover at least!* I sat down heavily on the bench. *Fuck!* All those nights buying coke from Dex, now wasted!

Two hours later, John, my UC handler, came to get me.

'Are you okay?' he asked as we left the station in his unmarked car.

'Yeah, I'm fine, John, but I was not expecting that. I wouldn't mind a heads-up next time TSG are going to raid the place I'm working.'

'We didn't know it was going to happen, Danni. It was a fuck up. They didn't do the proper checks. If they'd cross-checked on the system they would have seen our operation. Now they've gone and ruined a decent job. TSG – they're notorious for this kind of crap.'

'I was getting on so well tonight, too. I nutted into the main dealer.'

'Fuck!' John slammed his palm on the wheel. 'I cannae believe it. We were sitting waiting for you to come back and when you didn't appear at the safety location we realized something must have happened. That's when we found out the thickies had gone in . . .'

'I would have got more out of him if I had the time.'

'Aye, well, you dinnae need to bother now. It's finished.'

The pub was shut down immediately after the raid – probably due to the amount of damage caused by TSG! – so my job was over before I got a chance to nut into the real dealer. I was gutted. I didn't much enjoy getting arrested either, though it was interesting to be on the other side of the things during a raid. I couldn't for the life of me under-stand why the TSG officers had been so heavy-handed. Curious, I read their report afterwards and one claimed he smashed the bottles because they could have posed a safety risk if someone grabbed one to use as a weapon. *Rubbish!* Nobody had made any move towards those bottles, nobody acted defensively or aggressively. TSG were a liability – they gave coppers a bad name and put proper investigations in jeopardy. Apparently the dog never came back either, which was sad.

At least on that occasion the job had gone awry because of someone else's mistake. Worse was when I screwed things up. It didn't happen often – you couldn't afford to make mistakes in covert work or you wouldn't last long – but on one job in north London I got cocky and slipped up. I'd been buying from a woman called Mary in a crack den in Tottenham for a few weeks and things were going so well we decided to piggy-back in another TP – dealing to two of us was stronger in terms of evidence. It seemed pretty straight-forward. I'd been four times already and on each occasion it had run like clockwork. I'd go to the phone box at the end of the street, ring the mobile number, then Mary would come outside the house, serve up and leave. I was expecting the same again this time – but things didn't quite go according to plan.

I called the number as usual from the phone box to arrange a pick up and she told me I could come by the house. It was the ground-floor flat of a converted brick townhouse and me and the other TP went to meet her at the door, thinking we'd just get the stuff and go. But this time, when Mary opened the door and I told her I wanted 'two and two', she said: 'Yeah, come in.'

I shouldn't have agreed. That was my big mistake. I should have just stayed outside and done the deal on the doorstep, but I was a bit blasé by this point and I never thought anything would happen. So we stepped inside, following Mary, a small, skinny woman with dark frizzy hair and bad acne, through the corridor towards the living room, accompanied by the distinctive 'burning rubber' smell of crack.

In the grubby lounge there were three other people, lying on mattresses on the floor, apparently off their faces. Mary also looked like she'd smoked a fair bit today. Her pupils were enormous and her tiny body, encased in a grey vest top with no bra and tight jeans, twitched and jigged about.

'What do you want?' she said, plucking her stash from her back pocket.

'We want two each,' I said.

'Yeah, no worries,' she extracted four small cellophane-wrapped rocks and I prepared to hand over our money. But before she gave it to me she said: 'You can smoke in here.'

'Nah, I ain't smoking in here.'

'You are!' she insisted.

'Nah, I ain't,' I said again. The front door was behind us and she darted around both of us to block the way. Now, if we wanted to get to the front door, we were going to have to get past scary Mary somehow.

'You're smoking in here!' she grinned, manic eyes bulging, sweat beading at her forehead.

'No we're not,' I said again. 'Stop fucking around, Mary. Just give me the gear.'

'No. Smoke in here.'

'NO! Give me the fucking gear and get out the way of the fucking door.'

I could have grabbed her and pulled her away because she

was so small and frail-looking. I guessed she was about forty-five but she could have been twenty-five, for all I knew. Crack ages people. But I really didn't want to put my hands on her because it looked like she had been smoking all day and was behaving erratically. I had no idea how she would react if things turned physical. Neither could we rely on the three other people in the house to be on our side. I tried to weigh things up as rationally as I could: *Okay, so getting trapped in a crack den isn't ideal but she seems too wired to have any sort of game plan. It looks like she's just buzzing, her companions have passed out and she needs new party pals.*

'Fine – if you're not going to give it to me just get out the way and I'll go somewhere else,' I said. There was a moment of silence as she realized I was serious and about to leave. The party was over. She rolled her eyes and reluctantly handed over the crack. I slapped the notes in her hand angrily and shouldered past her towards the door, my nervous partner close at my heels. As I opened the door we were hit by a dazzling ray of sunlight and a wave of relief. *Fuck! That was close.* She probably wouldn't have hurt us unless she had weapons but, without doubt, that had been a monumentally stupid mistake on my part and totally avoidable. I was kicking myself all the way back to the safety location. *Why did you agree to go into the house? You should have said you had a cab waiting or that you had to meet someone.* My overconfidence had led to a very difficult situation, putting our deployment in jeopardy, and dragging a relatively inexperienced TP into something which could very easily have turned nasty.

Back at the station I took extra care in writing up the report. This wasn't the usual pick-up, which was over within ten minutes. I had to admit that we'd gone inside the house where she had wanted us to stay and 'take part in the property', but I played down the drama of the moment and counted my lucky stars that we had managed to leave without a fight. It reminded me how quickly things could turn and served as a useful reminder not to take silly risks. The TP had been pretty shaken up by the confrontation and I was just lucky that the DI in charge of the case didn't really know our rules well enough to pull me up on my mistake. It was definitely a near miss and I knew I had got off lightly on that occasion. I made a firm resolution from that point not to be complacent. I loved my work with SCD10 and had every intention of sticking around for a long time to come.

12

UFO

Now that the custody arrangements were behind us, Tom and I had to disentangle our financial affairs. This time I wasn't up for the fight. Naturally, I wanted my fair share of the assets, especially since I had sold my first flat to buy the three-bedroom family home, but everything was so difficult with Tom that instead of insisting on what was rightfully mine, demanding my share of the house from the capital I had accrued from the sale of my first flat, I let him take the majority of our joint assets to secure a swift exit. It wasn't my finest hour, I have to confess, but I didn't have it in me to keep battling. I'd had enough. All I wanted now was to get out and start building a life for me and Amelia. Finally, we were divorced. It had taken years of struggle and stress and I felt beaten down by it all. I had made it through with my mind and body intact, but only just!

Taking all the UC jobs I was offered meant I sometimes worked multiple deployments in the same day: a job in the morning, my normal day job in the day and another in the evening. One Friday, I got a last-minute overtime offer in the borough of Hackney. It was double pay and I couldn't afford to say no.

'Mum, can you pick up Amelia this afternoon please? I've been called out on a job.'

'All right, what time will you be back?

'I'm not sure – it might be late but I'll call you.'

'That's fine. Don't worry. She can have a sleepover with her nana tonight.'

'Thanks, Mum. I really appreciate it.'

My parents had been amazing in the wake of my split with Tom, stepping in to help with the childcare when I needed to work. Though Dad had always been aware of my under-cover work, Mum was still none the wiser as to the nature of the 'overtime', and to her credit she never questioned me about it either. All she knew was that I was a single parent trying to make ends meet. 'If you wanted me to know you'd tell me,' she'd say. And that suited me fine. At least the job that evening was outside of my normal working hours, so I didn't need a sign off from Heather. It had been getting harder and harder lately to get her permission for my UC deploy-ments. Heather seemed to be going out of her way to be awkward about things.

I tried to reassure her that I would catch up with the work in my spare time. After all, the Misper investigations didn't need to be completed within specific hours – but this didn't seem to be enough for her, and on several occasions in recent months I'd had to go over her head to get clearance.

'Where are you going?' she'd asked pointedly one day as I prepared to leave for a BTP job.

'I can't tell you. I'm going to be deployed – that's all I can say.'

'You've got to tell me where you're going, Danielle.'

'I can't. You know I can't. I'm sorry.'

'Then I'm not going to let you go,' she'd retaliated. I'd sighed but said nothing. *This is getting silly. She knows very well I can't give her any details of my covert work and if she puts her foot down I'll just ring John.* She had become resentful and belligerent over my deployments and these pointless arguments were just awkward and unpleasant. I had to find a way to deal with the situation once and for all.

Thankfully, the night of the Hackney job I didn't need her permission to leave. I finished work at 5 p.m. as usual, retrieved my kitbag from my station locker and changed into my standard street clothes: grey-green anorak, grey tracksuit bottoms, Nike trainers and some baby oil at the roots of my slicked-back hair. Then I drove through the rush-hour traffic to Hackney Police Station. The officer in charge of the investigation was a relatively new DI. I hadn't worked for her before and I guessed this must be one of her first covert operations. It seemed a relatively straightforward street job – they'd got a number from a local snout for a dealer called 'Sunny' and all I had to do was try to score off him.

At the station we called Sunny from my dirty phone.

'Sunny? Is that you, mate?' I said when he picked up.

'Yeah . . .' he drawled, casually.

'It's Dee.'

'Ah, Dee! Y'all right?'

I took a chance, pretending we knew each other, and it worked. Either he was too out of it to realize he didn't know me or he was covering.

'Listen, Sunny, I need some thingy, yeah. Will you meet me?'

'Yeah yeah. Usual spot.'

'Nah nah . . .' That wasn't going to work since I had no idea where the usual spot was. 'Can we meet at Shoreditch Park? Bench by the memorial.'

'Yeah. No problem.'

'Twenty minutes, okay?'

'Yeah.'

We were on. I quickly made my way from the station on foot towards Shoreditch Park, while the surveillance team took up their positions a good distance away. They had to keep eyes on me to find out what this guy looked like. I hurried towards the park through a light, warm drizzle, head down, hands jammed into the pockets of my anorak. It was early June and though it was nearing 8 p.m. it was still light enough to get a good look at the people around. Hackney was all familiar territory for me – the only problem was that I had no idea what this guy looked like. I sat on a bench near the spot I'd suggested and scanned the park for likely suppliers. Young mothers pushed their toddlers in buggies, a group of teenagers puffed ostentatiously on cigarettes and a young couple whispered together on another bench. *Come on. Come on, Sunny. Show yourself.*

It didn't take long to spot him. A bald black man in his early forties, around six feet, sauntered towards me in a red hoodie and low-slung jeans. He seemed to be in no hurry at all and when he got close up I saw he had a crumpled face and rheumy, yellow eyes. *Shit, he looks messed-up.*

He eased himself down onto the bench beside me.

'Y'all right Dee?' Sunny spoke in a low, slow drawl, the kind of chilled-out voice that reminded me of long, boozy afternoons on the beach. He seemed to do everything slowly, which was unusual. When you're buying off the street everything was brisk and to the point. Nobody wants to hang around in that situation. But Sunny was different. He looked like he had all the time in the world – was he stoned or just laid-back? I couldn't tell. I told him I wanted 'two white' and very slowly he pulled his black leather man bag over onto his lap and counted out the crack into my hand. This guy really didn't seem to give a hoot who was looking. He moved like he was underwater. I shoved the small cellophane-wrapped rocks deep into the pocket of my green anorak, gave him twenty quid and jumped up.

'Thanks, Sunny. I'll call you, yeah?'

'Yeah, Dee. No worries,' he smiled absently, heaved himself off the bench and moseyed away. I scurried off back to the nick to write my notes. The DI in charge of the case was giddy with delight.

'That's great, Danielle,' she trilled. 'I think we'll go again tomorrow if you can make it?'

'Erm, yeah, that should be fine,' I said. It was unusual to go back again the following day. Would I really have got rid of that crack so quickly? I didn't care – this was her investigation and I couldn't afford to say no to double pay.

On my way home I called Mum. We agreed I'd pick Amelia up on Saturday morning so I could spend the day with her before dropping her back at 4 p.m. I felt guilty. Of course I did. There was nothing I wanted more than to spend every moment of the weekend with my daughter. I longed to be the sort of mum who baked cakes, volunteered for PTA events at school, whipped up delicious, healthy home-made meals every night and spent hours patiently going over her homework. But single parenthood didn't look like that. It was messy and chaotic. I was too tired to shop and cook properly so we often ate out, I only had time to drop her at the school gates before screeching off to work and her homework was often hurriedly completed in the car at the very last minute. It was a careful balancing act and I felt constantly pulled in two directions. At least she had a loving extended family who were there for her, and it gave me great peace of mind to know she was in the care of her adoring grandparents, who spoiled her rotten.

On Saturday evening I went back to Hackney and we ran the same operation again with Sunny, meeting on the bench in the park where he'd served up the previous evening. It ran like clockwork and the DI was so cock-a-hoop she asked if I could piggyback another officer into the deal the following day. The UC who came along for my third meeting with Sunny was called Josh.

'Sunny, man, this is Josh. Can you sort him out?'

'Yeah yeah yeah . . . what do you want?'

Sunny was so slow and laid-back I reckon I could have taken a whole UC team to this deal! At least now we had multiple buys from Sunny, proving that there was an established pattern of behaviour. We must have bought from Sunny around ten times in total before the DI decided she had enough evidence to make an arrest. Talk about being sure! I heard through the grapevine that she got into trouble with command for employing us all on double pay several days in a row for that job, but I guess she just got carried away. Covert work could do that to you.

Sunny struck me as a nice guy. It was a shame he was a drug dealer. The evidence we were getting on him would likely put him behind bars for a long time and I imagined this wouldn't be his first stretch either – you don't just wake up one day and become a crack dealer. But I don't know what happened to him because once my part of the operation was over I rarely had anything to do with the court cases. Our evidence was usually so overwhelming any decent defence lawyer would convince their client to take a guilty plea early to mitigate a long sentence. I usually found my work pretty exhilarating, but after buying from Sunny ten times in a row, I was bored. Once the initial excitement of making the job work had worn off, it was all far too easy. There was no tension in the deployment, no challenge. Josh and I ended up playing a silly game during the next few meetings with Sunny, daring each other to drop nonsense words into the conversation just to liven things up a bit. I got him to say 'Chewbacca' and 'Rumpelstiltskin', which made me giggle, especially since we were wired up and the surveillance team were listening in.

It was just as well things were about to move up a gear for me.

Shortly after the Sunny job ended, I took a call from John, who told me I needed to get to Liverpool Street Station for 6 p.m. the following day.

'What is it – a deployment?' I asked.

'Nah. You'll see when you get there.'

It was all very vague. *At least I don't have to try and get round Heather*, I thought as I left work the following evening. I changed out of my uniform and into my normal clothes; since this wasn't a deployment I had no reason to get myself street-ready. Maybe this was just a drink up with the UC crowd – a secret leaving do and they didn't want to have it at the usual place. There were a couple of bars that the team liked to go to in the area.

When I arrived at Bishopsgate Police Station I was shown into a boardroom where I was surprised to find two other TPs I recognized and two senior UCs who also worked as instructors at Hendon. We all nodded at one another but no one spoke. *What's happening?* I thought as I took a seat at the table. *What are we all doing here?* John arrived a few minutes later.

'Thanks for coming today,' he started. 'You three test purchasers have been specially selected to train for the next level of covert work. You have all excelled in the field, demonstrating your skill and ability to pull off complex and challenging jobs. Now we are looking for officers who can go one step further, joining Level Ones on longer-term immersion deployments.'

My heart jumped – was he inviting us to take the NUTAC course?

'Now, usually we would put you up for the NUTAC,' he went on. 'But there aren't any more courses due to run this year, so this is what we're calling a "bridge" to the NUTAC.

It's the next level up and if you pass the training today you will become an Undercover Foundation Officer, and we can deploy you for more challenging work. Can I assume that you are all interested in taking the course today?'

Well, I suppose if it wasn't the NUTAC this was the next best thing. I was in. I looked at the two other TPs and we all shrugged our assent.

'Undercover Foundation Officer . . .' The guy next to me spoke slowly. 'Does this mean we'll become UFOs?' We all cracked up, which was a relief. Until now it had all been very silent, very serious.

'Aye, aye . . . I know it's a stupid acronym,' John rolled his eyes. 'But it wasn't my fucking idea. Yes, Gavin, you'll be UFOs. Right, we only need you a few hours this evening so if anyone isn't up for it, feel free to leave.'

Nobody moved.

'Okay – let's get going.'

Over the next three hours the experienced UCs took it in turns to interrogate us in a series of rapid-fire interviews. Bizarrely, we all stayed in the same room, listening, as one by one they turned their attention on each of us. When it came to my turn I remained calm but laser-focused as the questions came thick and fast.

'Where are you from?'

'What's your name?'

'What's your age?'

'Have you got family?'

'Are you married? Got a boyfriend?'

'Where do you drink? Where do you go out?'

'You're from Essex? That means you're a bit of a slag. Are you a slag?'

This is weird. What is the point of just asking us questions? I wondered. *They must know we can all keep our cool under pressure or we wouldn't have got this far.*

Nevertheless, I concentrated hard, just waiting for the trick question that would trip me up. At Hendon we'd been taught to put our hands on our knees when we gave evidence in court so that we didn't wave our hands in a way that might look unprofessional or distracting to the jury. So I kept my hands on my knees the whole time. This was a high-pressure test and I didn't want to over-gesticulate or seem dramatic. After three hours they seemed to run out of questions and the intense inquisition came to an abrupt stop.

There was a minute of conferring before John declared: 'Congratulations! You've all passed.'

Then he invited us to the All Bar One down the road for a celebratory drink. I have to admit it was one of the stranger moments in my policing career. *What the hell was all that about?* I wondered later at home. Reading between the lines it sounded like they had jobs lined up and nobody suitable to do them, which meant they had to get us out into the field as quickly as possible. There was no time for a NUTAC so they hastily threw together this 'bridge' and sent the three of us over: one woman, a black guy and an officer with a Polish background. It looked like they were trying to diversify their pool of officers – and fast! I've certainly never heard of anyone else taking the 'bridge to the NUTAC' before or since.

Two days later I was deployed on a job with a Level One in Stratford.

'It's one night,' said John when he called me with the details. 'You don't have to say anything or do anything. We just need you to accompany our officer to a nightclub to give credibility to his legend that he is who he says he is and to be another pair of eyes on the ground. Is that okay?'

'I guess so,' I said, bemused.

'Look, Danielle, there isn't much for you to do here but make no mistake, this is a very sensitive operation. Christian has been on the job for a long time. He needs you to follow his lead and be there as another set of eyes and ears. Is that okay?'

That night I met up with the UC, a very experienced Level One officer who I'd seen a few times before at the pub. He had long hair and was wearing a black leather jacket and jeans. Christian was fluent in Russian and he gave me a very brief idea of what to expect when we went to the club.

'You don't need to say anything,' he explained. 'In fact it's better if you don't. The people we're meeting, they're not fucking around. Just let me do what I need to do and go with it.'

At 11 p.m. we drove through the backstreets of Stratford until we turned off into what looked like an old warehouse on a business estate. *This isn't a real, licensed nightclub*, I realized as we walked through the large gates and up the stairs towards a converted office. *More like an illegal drinking den.* Inside the massive warehouse two rooms had been turned into a makeshift bar with fluorescent strip lighting and dark satin sheets taped up on the walls and over the windows. There were sofas dotted around the concrete floor and most of the men were chomping on huge cigars. A very fat man spread out on a sofa was gnawing so hard on a giant Gauloise cigar it looked like he was going to eat it! Of the twenty-odd people in the room only around five were women. Most of the tables had vodka bottles on them. Christian spoke only Russian from the moment we arrived and I noticed that some of the guys he spoke to had tattoos with Cyrillic writing similar to ones on Christian's arms.

I teetered in on Christian's arm in my tight jeans and heels and did as I was instructed, looking dumb and pretty for as long as Christian needed me to. The people there were very nice and actually spoke to me respectfully rather than just looking me up and down. I was offered a few shots of vodka and made comfortable while Christian carried out his business dealings. It took around forty-five minutes and after they had concluded we left. In the car on the way back to the safety location I asked him what they'd talked about.

'A weapons deal,' he said. 'We're almost there. Next meeting is at the Roman baths in Canning Town. These guys prefer doing business with their clothes off cos they're paranoid someone might be wearing a wire. You coming to the next one?'

I laughed. It had been a real eye-opener tonight. And I was so impressed by Christian. His ability to move and operate among people who I assumed were high-level Russian mafiosi was truly awe-inspiring. And I know this might sound naive but, before then, I had never met anyone who could speak Russian who wasn't Russian. I was aware it was a very tricky language to learn, let alone to speak fluently enough to convince Russian natives that he was one of them. This guy was working at a level I'd never seen before.

He was in deep, dangerous waters and one wrong word in the company of these people could prove lethal. I'd heard other UC officers talk about Christian before and assumed that the way they referred to him as a 'genius' and 'one of a kind' was probably a little overblown. Now I knew why they spoke of him in such glowing terms. I found out he'd gone to secondary school at the age of ten and also spoke French, Spanish, German and Italian as well as some other Eastern European languages. For a cockney like me – a real one, mind, as I was born within the sound of the Bow Bells – speaking one other language besides English was mind-blowing, let alone five! He was clever, accomplished and utterly fearless. I reckoned I could learn a lot from him and hoped we would be deployed together on more jobs in the future. Now that I was a UFO I was ready to take the next step in my career . . .

13

Going Deeper

As I stepped into the lobby of the dingy hostel in Victoria I was struck by a weird and unpleasant smell. *What is that? Dirt mingled with custard?* It was like a million bad smells from the past combined with freshly created odours; layers of dirt, spillages and carpet stains built up over decades. *God, they need to knock this place down and start again*, I thought as I moved through to the ancient lounge area. It was like stepping back in time. Old-fashioned flowered wallpaper, peeling at the edges, hung on the walls around sagging armchairs and chipped wooden tables. Nobody had changed a lightbulb – or a lampshade, for that matter – since the seventies, so the bad lighting was punctured occasionally by the odd flicker. Stale smoke hung in the air, attached to the furniture. It was just about the most depressing place I'd ever been in and worse, it was boiling hot.

Funnily enough, Christian was the officer in charge of this job and he'd requested that I come on board to help them infiltrate a drugs network operating in this area. This cheap and downtrodden hostel was a popular hangout for local addicts and usually awash with drugs. The issue was finding the right person to approach. I'd dressed down in a pale-blue vest top and tatty jeans, with my usual green anorak. The heat completed the look, making my hair frizzy at the ends and super greasy at the roots. Now I loitered in the lounge of the hostel for ages, quietly watching the ebb and flow of visitors, before choosing a particularly dishevelled-looking fellow sitting in the corridor, swigging red wine from a bottle. I gave him a surreptitious nod as I sidled up to him.

'Y'all right?' I said.

'Aye, not bad,' he sniffed, offering me the bottle. I politely declined.

'You got a light?'

'Yeah, sure. You got a smoke for me too?'

I pulled out my pack of Silk Cut Lights and we went to sit on the steps outside the hostel for a smoke, talking shit for a while. I couldn't go straight in and ask who was serving up. It would have been too obvious. So we just sat and chatted for a while.

My new friend was clearly a popular guy and some other people came over to chat. They were mostly other residents in the hostel – many of them looked very rough and one or two had cans of lager while one guy kept scratching his legs.

'Bloody scabies,' he muttered as he itched his calf. I tried to stand well back from him! Eventually I got the subject onto who was serving up and my friend with the red wine said he knew somebody we could call. Maybe she could help us out, maybe not, but either way he'd only call her if I could chip him off. You don't get something for nothing in this world! I agreed and he made the call.

Half an hour later we found ourselves trudging through

the backstreets of Victoria to a bleak, high-rise estate where kids who should have been at school wheeled around on bikes and bags of rubbish poured out of overflowing bins. This was a part of London where the deprived areas sat side by side with the richest, so even though it was grubby and unkempt, you could turn a corner and find yourself staring at the beautifully maintained courtyard of an upmarket, luxury development. We pushed our way through a group of bored-looking teens and up the stairwell of one council block to a second-floor flat. To my surprise a girl came to the door who looked no more than sixteen. A very young sixteen, at that.

'What can I get you?' she asked in a cut-glass English accent. *What the hell is this girl doing here?* I wondered. She was young, pretty, well-spoken and very wholesome. She wouldn't look out of place at a sailing regatta, but here she seemed totally incongruous.

'Two and two,' I said. She pulled the wraps from her back pocket and handed them to me. There was something in the way she moved and acted that told me she had come from a wealthy family. Her long, honey-streaked hair shone, she had that fresh-faced look of a kid who had spent a lot of time with a hockey stick in her hand, and generally everything about her seemed healthy and well-cared for. This was a girl who had never had to hustle a day in her life. Her presence was an anomaly.

Once I'd established that she was the dealer for the area, I got the girl's number from my friend and went back a few times to buy from her again. I couldn't shake the feeling that something was seriously amiss here and I wanted to know what it was. On my fourth visit she didn't have enough crack in her back pocket so she called out: 'Dylan!'

'What?' a deep male voice shouted back.

'I need some more.'

'Yeah, all right,' he called back and then this tall guy in his early thirties appeared from the living room. He bowled up behind her and slipped something into her hand before whispering something into her ear while stroking her hair in a way that clearly indicated he was her boyfriend. She let a fleeting smile cross her lips before turning back to me and rearranging her features into a blank mask again. *Ah, so you're the real dealer*, I thought. This kid had been groomed and set up to act as the front person for his operation so that he didn't have to get his hands dirty. He most certainly knew the law – and she didn't – which meant that she was the one taking all the risk.

Back at the station we ran some searches and found that the girl had been reported missing some months earlier by her father, a wealthy businessman. Now she was almost certainly facing a lengthy prison sentence while her 'boyfriend' would get off scot-free. It really upset me. It wasn't the first time I'd come across young kids in the drugs world but I felt there was something so sinister about what I had witnessed. This girl had probably been duped into thinking this guy was really into her, and that they were a couple, rather than the cold, hard reality which is that she had been set up as the stooge. He had used her innocence and naivety to carry out his illicit business dealings and, once he'd used and abused her, would no doubt find some other young victim to prey upon.

'I don't like seeing young girls getting mixed up like that,' I told Christian during 'celebratory' drinks one Friday after the job ended. 'It doesn't sit right with me. She was probably underage when she fell for the wrong bloke and now her life is going to be ruined.'

'Bad choices,' Christian said thoughtfully. 'It's not up to us to help other people make the right decisions in life. It's up to us to stop criminal activity. She knew enough – she could have walked out at any time, gone back home and returned to her clearly privileged life. At least she started out with chances and opportunities. Most of the adults we deal with – who were all kids once – had nothing like the same life chances. She had everything on a plate. We found the supply and stopped it. Job done.'

'Hmm . . .' I suppose he was right. I'd seen enough kids dragged into gang culture to know that they had no choice, it was simply a matter of survival. She had the choice. But still, I felt a niggling discomfort. Was she really a criminal or a victim? We may have shut down the supply for a while but, since we didn't have anything on the bloke, it was only a matter of time before he set up another operation elsewhere. It's not like we were stopping drugs getting to the streets altogether, just temporarily halting the flow.

'Anyway, you did a great job, Danni,' Christian grinned. 'Well done. Cheers to you!'

I allowed myself a little smile and graciously accepted the toast. It meant a lot coming from Christian. He was greatly admired among our group, performing his job to the highest standard. I'd even hear people say that he was the best UC they'd ever had and I thought that, if I could learn from him, I would only improve. I was so fascinated by him and I liked to pump him for information on the jobs he'd done and the work he was doing now.

'What about the tattoos?' I asked him one night.

'They're Russian prison tattoos,' he explained.

'Why have you got them?'

'Well, I speak and read Russian and I'm really into tattoo art. I just like them, I suppose. They certainly don't hurt in the circles I move in.'

We were deployed together a couple more times after that and found that we worked very well as a team. Neither of us had any inhibitions – we just said and did what came naturally in the moment. It felt really easy. I'd noticed that some UCs were a bit hesitant in the field, always second-guessing themselves, so I found myself overcompensating for their shiftiness, instead of just being natural. Some even tried to work out a script beforehand, giving out instructions: 'You say this and I'll say that.' It drove me mad.

'No, I don't want a script. It will come off as fake. Let's just go and do it,' I argued. Scripts couldn't work. You didn't know what was going to happen so you couldn't plan what to say or do. You just had to go with it and adapt to every changing situation in an authentic way. I had certain things I knew could fall back on, but I never knew which reaction or response to employ until I was there in the moment.

If someone wanted to chip off I'd be tying my shoelaces or

preoccupied with my phone when they asked to ensure that I didn't have to do it for them, avoiding the pitfall of potentially being accused of supplying myself. If someone asked me to 'mouth it' – which meant putting the cellophane-wrapped crack in your mouth to avoid detection – I'd find a way to hide it elsewhere. One lady used to keep her supply inside a plastic Kinder egg which she kept inside her privates. When you bought from her, she'd cock her leg, pop out the egg, crack it open and give you the rock – crack from her crack! Then she instructed me to 'mouth it'. Now, there are a lot of things I was prepared to do in my line of work, but I did not have it in me to put that little pack of crack in my mouth, so I just said, 'Yeah yeah yeah . . .' while sliding it into my pocket. The next time I bought off her I made sure I was eating an apple so she wouldn't tell me to mouth it. Normally, a desperate user will do whatever they're told and if I'm told to chuck it in my mouth I'll do it, clenching it between my teeth so it doesn't touch the insides of my mouth. You don't know where it's been! But in this case, I couldn't. Everyone has their limits and this was mine.

Christian was also very good at thinking on his feet and I found that our work in the field was characterized by each of us listening carefully to the other and responding to what they said. If I was talking he was listening and vice versa. There was no worry about getting it wrong. I knew what was going on all the time and moved with the flow.

To be honest, I didn't want to have to deal with someone else's legend and for that reason I mostly preferred to work on my own. Apart from Christian there were just a couple of other UCs I liked to work with.

Occasionally, I was called in to jobs where other UCs had been 'bounced', which meant they were unsuccessful for one reason or another. For one particular job in north-east London, I was asked to see if I could infiltrate an organized crime group from Turkey. They operated out of the back of a snooker club and two UCs had already been sent packing.

'You might not have any luck here,' said John when he called with the details. 'Two of our guys have already tried the buzzer for the club and were told to "fuck off back to the police station". It wouldn't surprise us if they bounced you too. These guys seem to have a highly attuned nose for covert officers.'

I took the job, of course, because I love a challenge but as the day approached, I began to feel apprehensive. I had never been in a position where I had failed to come back with the product. On this occasion it was just weed but we knew that the snooker hall was a front for other gang-related activity so we needed to start buying to establish a connection.

It was a hot summer's day and I was wearing a bright pink and orange summer dress when I approached the locked door off the main road and buzzed the buzzer.

'Yeah, what is it?' a man's voice answered.

'I'm here to pick up,' I replied, and he let me in. Once I was through the first door I found myself in a more or less empty room with just a snooker table in the middle, without any snooker balls or cues, so I walked over to another door on the other side of the room where there was another buzzer and a camera. I buzzed and was let in. I was now in a tiny hallway between two locked doors and at the end there was a hatch. *Fantastic – I'm in!* The guy opened the hatch and asked me what I wanted. I said twenty. He passed me the weed – job done!

I went back a few more times to score and eventually he opened the door instead of just the hatch. Now I could see into the main operation room for the gang. This was a serious set-up – there was a whole bank of CCTV screens monitoring the entire area surrounding the place. There were other guys in there chilling, piles of cash, a few phones and a couple of firearms casually laid on tables. They all seemed really laid-back, not at all bothered that I was there. The guy who I'd been dealing with – Emer – told me to take his number, suggesting we should link up. Emer was tall and tanned with dark hair and he wore a white vest with a gold chain around his neck. He wasn't bad looking and probably around twenty-five. But his suggestion made me uncomfortable. I took the number and knew I would hear from him. It didn't take long and he was calling and texting. I tried to get him to back off by saying that I had a boyfriend but this didn't deter him one bit.

'I'd make a better boyfriend,' he laughed.

I went back to get product multiple times and each time Emer would open the door to me, so I stayed as long as I could to soak up the intel. This could be anything that could prove useful to the investigation – who was in there, what they looked like, what cars they might be driving. Even their footwear, what they were eating, what fags they smoked. Eventually I was comfortable enough to wear a recording device, which I sewed into my dress myself. I always preferred to do my own kit because I knew what worked and what didn't. I'd replace one of the buttons on my top with a buttonhole camera, then I'd run the wire along the bottom of my bra and the pack would sit nicely at the back. It was comfortable enough for a short time but, if I was wearing it for extended periods, the pack got so hot it actually hurt.

I went back a couple more times with the camera until the officer in charge had enough evidence to make the arrest. Now a huge team of armed officers gathered, being careful to stay well clear of all the CCTV cameras in order to avoid detection. This was my final deal and I had mixed feelings. On the one hand I felt bad knowing that Emer's entire world was about to change. He didn't have a clue when he woke up that morning that it would end up with him in prison. At the same time, I was pleased to be ending this criminal operation. The weed was just the tip of the iceberg. These guys were involved in far more serious crime, like human trafficking and prostitution rings. Breaking up this gang would at least put a stop to their illegal trade in human misery.

I went in as usual, bought the drugs and walked out, letting the team know who was in there and what they had on them. Forewarned was forearmed. I was just finishing up the briefing when Emer called on my mobile.

'Enough's enough,' he said. 'You've got to let me take you out—'

'POLICE POLICE POLICE. DON'T MOVE!'

And with that I heard the sound of the raid through his phone as the arrest team went in. *Well, that was the last time I'd be hearing from him, thank god!* It had been a very successful operation with multiple charges on all the gang members including violent crimes, illegal arms and sex crimes, to which they pleaded guilty.

It was a job worth celebrating, and Christian was one of the first to congratulate me at the next UC meet-up. We kept bumping into each other at the pub and gradually, over time, we learned a little more about each other. It seemed we had more in common than just our work. He was ten years my senior and, in a similar way to me, he was just dealing with the disintegration of a serious, long-term relationship. Like me, I think he found work to be a useful distraction from the difficulties in his personal life. We were just mates to begin with but a lot of our colleagues started to refer to us as 'work husband and wife' and the more we worked and socialized, the closer we got. People assumed from the start that we were going out but it didn't happen right away. There was certainly no big 'aha' moment, no staring soulfully into each other's eyes; it just sort of happened. One Friday night, at the usual UC get-together, we had been talking and drinking for hours when, just as we were about to say good-night, we leaned in and our lips met. A week later we went out for dinner and afterwards he came back to my place. Just like with our work, it felt easy, natural and right. Christian and I understood each other. Our relationship was built on trust and respect – he could read me and I could do the same for him. For the first time in years I felt my partner really had my back.

14

Guns and Paedophiles

It was late on a Friday afternoon in 2010 when I got the call to come up to the Yard.

'What is it?' I asked John. It was close to 3 p.m. which meant calling either Mum or Dad to step in at the last minute to collect Amelia from school.

'CO14 have a job for you but it's time-sensitive and we need you up here as quick as you can.'

'Right. I'll try and be there in forty-five minutes, one hour tops.'

'Aye, I'll let them know.'

CO14 were still a relatively new unit tackling sexual offences and my dealings with them had been quite limited until now. I primed my mum, got permission to leave and headed up to Scotland Yard.

At the Yard, I was briefed by the CO14 team, one of whom was a strapping grey-haired DC. He'd been communicating with a suspected paedophile in a chat room for the last couple of weeks, posing as a fourteen-year-old schoolgirl. This was a fairly new technique – of course since then chat rooms and forums have been surpassed by social media – but at this time very few investigations involved infiltrating the online communities where paedophiles preyed. The team handed over a whacking great pile of pages.

'What's this?'

'That's the manuscript of the chat so far. We need you to read it so you're all up to speed on everything that has been said because we want you to go face to face with him.'

'When?'

'In an hour.'

I took a look at the stack of papers I was being asked to read and digest. *An hour? Shit! Better crack on!*

The team had set up a video call between me – posing as Sophie, the fourteen-year-old created by the DC – and David, a known paedophile who seemed to be trying to ensnare his next victim. I sat down in the room and skimmed the online chats. They had started out as fairly mundane conversations with discussions about how each other's day had been, what had irritated them, how they enjoyed playing a certain game online. But within a few days David started asking very personal questions: her bra size, whether she had ever had a boyfriend, if she liked older men. Now he wanted to see her face in a video call because, apparently, and this sentence surprised me: '. . . you never know, there could be police on here.'

So David was suspicious but not enough to stop him from following through on his urges. He just wanted to make sure the DC wasn't a copper. Well, I was only too happy to put his mind at rest! Of course I was in my twenties at this point – and a mother myself – so I did what I could to make my appearance seem more youthful. I tied my hair back in a plait and removed all my make-up. Someone found a white shirt for me in M & S so I could appear to have come from school and since the video camera was only on my upper half, I left my bottom half in uniform.

By 4.30 p.m., I was sat at the laptop, ready to take the Skype call, with three CO14 officers opposite me, off camera, taking notes and prepared to give directions when I needed them. Behind me was a white wall and I sat with the laptop on my lap so David couldn't see anything other than me in shot.

The call came through and I was met with a fifty-year-old male with grey straggly hair and wide-rimmed glasses. He seemed very pleased to see me.

'Hello, Sophie!' he grinned.

'Oh, hello David . . .' I tried to sound as young as I could, adding a nervous hesitancy to my delivery and keeping my voice high.

'How are you?' I said politely.

'I'm all right. What you been up to?'

'I just got home from school,' I said. I had been told to say quite clearly that I was at school to ensure he was in no doubt that I was a child. We chatted casually for a while, he told me that he'd been at work and it was very boring but that he'd been thinking about me all day and that's what made the time pass quicker.

There was a pause and then he said coyly: 'I've got something for you.'

'Oh really? Nah, you don't have to buy me anything,' I said naively.

'Are you watching?'

'Yeah.'

And he undid his trousers on camera and started masturbating. *Bloody hell!* I quickly slammed down the lid, then burst out laughing.

'What? What's he doing?' the DC asked.

'He's wanking on the camera!'

'Why did you shut the lid?'

'I don't want to see that! How am I supposed to respond?'

'This is perfect!' the DC said. 'He thinks you're a fourteen-year-old and this could be valuable evidence – we need to try and get it all recorded. Call him back and see if he'll do it again.'

So I rang him back.

'Did you see?' he said, a little out of breath, all pleased with himself. 'I did that for you. I did that for you, Sophie.'

'What did you do? I didn't see anything.' I played dumb.

'What do you mean?'

'I didn't see it. Just do it again.'

At that he got really angry with me.

'I can't do it again! I did it for you. Why didn't you see it?'

'My mum came in so I had to close the computer.'

'Oh, I see. Yeah, well, you don't want her to know about us. Not yet. We can tell her in time but now she might not understand our special friendship and she might stop you from talking to me. You don't want that, do you?'

'No, I don't.'

'Neither do I. So let's not tell her, yeah?

We chatted a little longer. It turned out David couldn't give me his 'gift' a second time, so soon after the first, which I have to say was quite a relief, but in any case he said he'd much rather give me a 'treat' in person.

'Let's meet next week,' he suggested.

'Okay – after school?' The conversation was being recorded, of course, so for the benefit of the recording, I made extra sure to drop in a few more school references.

'No. What about Tuesday? Don't go to school. I'll meet you outside Finchley Central tube station and we'll go out for the day. I'll bring you a present.'

Urgh! The thought of facing David and his horrid, wrinkly penis in real life sent shivers up my spine, but of course I played along and agreed readily to the arrangement.

Once we finished the call the CO14 team were delighted. This was exactly what they needed to make the arrest. The DC continued to communicate online as 'Sophie' and confirmed their arrangement. On the day, David came from his home in Welwyn Garden City all the way into town to meet with 'Sophie', which was in itself an offence: travelling with the intent to solicit a minor. Then, when he got to the station they nicked him and he was convicted of a number of offences, including possession of indecent images of a minor but also Section 14 of the Sexual Offences Act 2003, which states that it is an offence to arrange a meeting, or to facilitate a meeting, with a child under the age of sixteen with the intent of sexually abusing the child or with the intent of another person sexually abusing them. The evidence was quite overwhelming.

*

179

More and more of our work was being set up online, and that included our dealings with some of the serious gang-related crime rife in London. Another UC, a Level One, had been involved in setting up a gun deal in north London, making all the arrangements on Myspace. They just needed to bring in another UC to put another set of eyes on the ground and substantiate what happened.

I arrived at Enfield station, where the UC gave me a very quick run-down of what had been said online. He was buying a handgun and we would go down to the pick-up point and make the transaction. So we arrived in the car park of a block of local-authority flats. It was in a quiet residential area where nobody noticed or cared what we were doing. At the far end of the car park was the blue Toyota we'd been told to look out for. The driver signalled for us to come closer and we walked over. I knew the UC officer well and had worked with him and for him on several occasions. He was really experienced so I didn't have any qualms about following his lead and when we were directed to get in the car, I did it without question. Strictly speaking, of course, we were breaking an important rule, but you had to do that sometimes. I guessed he wasn't going to hand over the gun in full view of the public. Sometimes, the way the rules were set out and the way things happened in reality didn't always match up. In the moment you had to make a split-second judgement and just hope that you called it right.

The two of us got in the back seat and two blokes in the front seat looked round at us. They were both white, early thirties, and they seemed to do a very quick assessment of us both.

'All right?'

'Yeah, you got it?'

The man in the passenger seat pulled a handgun out from the glove box and handed it over. My fellow officer took hold of it and started examining it, clipping and unclipping it, looking down the sight and generally checking it over. He knew what he was looking for and was clearly satisfied with the product, so he got out a large wad of notes and handed them over to the guy in the front seat to count. It looked like a few hundred quid to me. I did my best to look bored and disinterested, though inside I was giddy with excitement. We were buying a gun! I wondered where it had been before and if it had been used.

'Yeah, yeah . . . this is fine,' said the officer. 'Can you get any others?'

'Let us know if you need anything and we'll work it out.'

'Wicked.' And with that he nodded at me, we got out the car, climbed into ours and drove back to the station. A fire-arms officer was there to meet us and book in the weapon. I wasn't even allowed to touch it. The job had gone smoothly and now we knew this was an established supply they would probably buy more to build up the evidence.

Apart from the paedophiles – who generally operated alone – most of the people we dealt with were gang-related in some way, whether that was for guns, drugs or prostitution. And for the most part the people we caught were on the bottom rung of the ladder. The gang leaders, the only ones it would make a real difference if you got, were businessmen. They were smart and nimble, experts in keeping themselves removed from criminal activity. These guys didn't get their hands dirty because, for the most part, they were also running largely legal businesses they could run all this dirty money through. These guys weren't on the streets, they were managing bars or coffee shops, restaurants, laundrettes or nightclubs. The money that came through their gangs all needed a front business or they wouldn't be able to live the lifestyle that the cash afforded them. I knew that some UCs were trying to reach further up the ladder through long-term infiltration, to catch these guys, but more often than not we had to satisfy ourselves with the low-hanging fruit. At least with paedophiles, you knew that once you'd caught them their activity was stopped. Nobody was going to take their place or carry out offences for them.

CO14 had been so pleased with my work that they drafted me again quite quickly. They had their sights on a paedophile who had already spent time in prison. As part of his bail conditions, Robert wasn't allowed access to any technical kit. He couldn't even own a computer. But of course it had only been a matter of months before he broke his bail requirements, buying himself a second-hand computer, and he was now roving around online, searching for his next victim. Once again, I was tapped up to do the 'identification' video call and it was a similar scenario to David. Robert wanted to see me on camera so I donned my schoolgirl uniform and 'met' him on Skype. He was a slim man in his late sixties with a few front teeth missing, wearing grubby, stained clothes. The look on his face when he saw me was one of pure delight.

Once again I played the innocent schoolgirl, repeatedly

dropping references to my school into the conversation. He had previously asked for a photo of me and, because the team wanted him to believe I was a real person, they asked if I would be okay to provide an actual school photo. I didn't mind in the least. I wanted to catch this bastard. Subsequently, the team established a 'pool' of photos of officers when they were younger to be used by the CO14 unit for catching paedophiles. Robert seemed incredibly keen to meet in person, and this time CO14 asked me to come to the meeting point, as they feared he might bolt if he didn't see me there.

On the day, Robert travelled from his home in Ipswich all the way to London Liverpool Street. I was waiting for him on the station concourse as his train pulled in, dressed in jeans and a jacket. It was freezing cold and the wind kept whacking me as it swooshed around the station. Still, this was worth getting cold for. As soon as the doors opened and all the passengers got out, I spotted him. He was small and slim with thinning grey hair he'd combed over his head, glasses and one of those horrible patterned jumpers people wore in the seventies. It was dirty and disgusting, as if he hadn't washed it in all that time either. *God, he actually looks like a stereotypical paedophile*, I thought to myself.

His face broke out in a massive smile when he saw me and he waved happily in my direction. Poor Robert looked as if he would burst with joy as he shuffled his way towards me, past the barriers and through the busy concourse. And that's when the team jumped him. Six burly officers tackled him to the floor, while I just carried on walking as if I'd never seen him. He was blindsided and as I strode purposefully in the opposite direction, I heard his pathetic cries and protestations of innocence while the officers put him in cuffs and walked him out – and back to jail. *Gotcha!*

Annoyingly, Robert pleaded 'not guilty' to the charge, so we had to go to Southwark Crown Court, where I gave my evidence. Of course, Robert never knew I was a copper, not until the moment I took the stand. And it was only when I started recounting our interactions – when he saw my face and heard my voice – that the penny dropped. He gaped in disbelief, then his face crumpled as he realized I was not a little girl after all. He appeared devastated, heartbroken even, and I'm sure that his reactions did not go unnoticed by the jury. As I left the stand I felt a real sense of pride and accomplishment. He was found guilty and sent back to prison, which was the right thing. He was clearly still a serious risk to children and I was glad that I'd been instrumental in putting him away.

I liked these jobs. We were actually taking dangerous predators off the streets. It wasn't always video calls. Sometimes I'd be asked to take a standard telephone call with the suspect and on those occasions CO14 might come to me. I'd read the transcripts of the online chats then we'd quickly make and record the phone call. I tried not to dwell, not to take my work home with me; I just dealt with the task in hand and moved swiftly onto the next job. The one time I felt a lingering disgust about dealing with a suspect was when we turned over a paedophile who had done some truly horrendous stuff. The officer in charge called to tell me they'd nicked the guy and when they searched his house in Essex they had found footage of him abusing babies. That was so twisted, so horrifying that I felt sick to my stomach for a week. My one consolation was that at least we had stopped him in his tracks, though tragically it had come too late for some victims.

Meanwhile, things were going well in my private life, for a change! My relationship with Christian was a breath of fresh air – easy, comfortable, trusting. Everything felt different with Christian. I didn't have to lie or hide anything because he was a part of the undercover world, so we talked freely about our jobs. I could even ask his advice on certain jobs and he would let me know whether he knew the team or the type of work involved. I felt confident in this relationship, comfortable being myself. I was older, wiser and more in control than before and enjoyed being appreciated too. Christian didn't just know about the work I did, he knew I was good at it, and having his admiration and respect made a big difference. While I was out on the street I didn't think about the risks, but afterwards it was nice to hear that I'd done a good job. No one in our unit was surprised we got together and nobody minded either. Our relationship came naturally in all areas.

Then, eight months into seeing Christian, during a girls' trip up to Liverpool, one of my girlfriends observed: 'Your boobs are huge, Danni!'

'No they're not!'

'They are.'

I looked down – *God, she's right, they are. And actually, they're a bit sore. Oh god. Oh god!*

I did the test that night and it came back positive. I was pregnant. It was a shock.

I had assumed that Amelia would be an only child. I didn't think about having any more children and Christian already had two boys from his previous relationship so neither of us was looking to expand our families. But I wasn't upset. When I examined my feelings I found I was actually quite excited about having another baby. I had just never imagined that one day I would have two children from two different fathers. It was a normal and accepted part of life, of course, but I guess I had never imagined that situation for me. *Get over yourself*, I told myself. *Nobody has a 'normal' family or a 'normal' relationship. You should know by now there's no such thing!* Perhaps, because of my past, I'd idealized the notion of a 'traditional family', which was how I'd got into such a pickle with my marriage. But it was time to let that go, time to discard those preconceived and childish notions of a traditional family unit and just live my life.

My only worry now was telling Christian. After all, it was still a fairly new relationship. Fortunately, he was very level-headed about it.

'That's fine,' he smiled, taking me into a big hug. 'We'll deal with it together.'

The next step was telling Amelia, who was now nearly seven years old. There would be quite an age gap and I worried about how she'd feel. I didn't want her to feel pushed to one side. Thankfully, I needn't have worried. Amelia was absolutely fine with the news and more excited than any of us. She couldn't wait to become a big sister. By now, my little girl was really coming into her own. She excelled in sport and had a very competitive streak. The kid could run! She was bright too, always doing well at school. Thankfully, she had inherited a little height from her dad so she wasn't tiny like me! And I was grateful that she had been so young when Tom and I split, so she didn't have too many bad memories. Best of all, she was a lovely person with a kind and grateful outlook. I loved spending time with her. And the more I thought about it, the more I felt she'd be a great sibling.

15

From Crack to Chrysanthemums

'I'm sorry but we can't find a heartbeat . . .' said the doctor gently.

'What? What does that mean?' I was confused. I was twenty-eight years old and although this was another unplanned pregnancy, I had come round to the idea over the past few weeks and was now pleased to be having another baby. Christian was a great guy and he was excited about becoming a dad again. Thankfully, I'd had no issues in the early weeks – no sickness or discomfort – and had gone along for my twelve-week scan at Whipps Cross Hospital alone, expecting to be told my due date and sent on my way. At first, everything was normal. I lay back on the table, pulled my top up and the sonographer smeared jelly over my bump before holding the sonic device on my skin and moving it around. The grainy image appeared on the screen and she squinted at it, frowning without speaking. Eventually she said: 'Just bear with me one minute,' and left the room, returning a minute later with a doctor.

By now I was beginning to feel worried. The doctor moved the handheld scanner over my belly for a couple more minutes, her eyes fixed to the screen, before telling me that there was no heartbeat. I didn't understand.

'Unfortunately, it looks like the baby's died,' she said.

'Oh . . .' I didn't know what to say. 'What do I do now, then?'

'Well, we need to talk about removing what is still there.'

I was in shock and was starting to feel shaky and alone.

'Erm, well, can I call my partner? I think I need to speak to him first.'

'Sure, why don't you go home and we'll bring you back in a couple of days.'

I don't recall what happened next – I was in such a state. All I knew was that the baby who I'd never expected was now dead inside me. How did it happen? *Why* did it happen? Was it my fault? I called Christian and he came to meet me at the hospital. By the time I got home I was in floods of tears.

'It happens,' Christian tried to comfort me as I wiped away the tears. 'We know the stats – one in four pregnancies end in miscarriage. It's very common.'

'I know. I know it is,' I nodded. 'It happens to people all the time. There's no reason it shouldn't happen to me too. I'm a realist. I get it.'

A heavy silence fell between us.

'It doesn't make it easier, does it?' he said forlornly.

'No, it doesn't. I just thought – I don't know, this probably sounds silly – but I thought I'd know if something happened to the baby. I thought I'd be able to tell. Why didn't I feel something? Does that make me a bad mother?'

'Of course not. You mustn't blame yourself.'

'I just want to know what happened.'

Christian shook his head.

'We'll probably never know and, to be honest, we shouldn't drive ourselves mad trying to figure it out. All we can say for sure is that it wasn't a viable pregnancy. Better to know now than to find out further along. The point is, Danni, you can get pregnant again, we know that, so it doesn't mean it will never happen. Let's just get through this and then we can think about trying again.'

'You'd like to?'

'Sure. I wanted this baby too.'

It was a heartbreaking time. I thought hard of how to tell Amelia and in the end decided to wait until it was all over and I could trust myself not to burst into tears in the middle of our discussion. *She's going to be devastated and right now I don't think I can take it.* I was grieving, not just for the child inside me who I'd started to love, but for all of us and how our family would never know this little person. As much as I tried not to overthink it, I lay awake at night, wondering if it was something I had done that caused the foetus to die. It was pointless, of course. As Christian pointed out, we'd probably never know, but it didn't stop me wondering.

Two days later, Christian accompanied me back to Whipps Cross hospital for the 'removal' – I'd read the literature they'd given me at the hospital and looked up the details online. As far as I understood it, I had to take a couple of pills that would make the lining of my womb contract, causing cramping and bleeding, similar to a natural miscarriage. I was trying to look on the bright side – at least it wasn't an invasive procedure, just a couple of pills. Nothing to fear and, according to the pamphlets I'd read, it should all be over within forty-eight hours. I was ready and, to be honest, I just wanted to get it over with. Not long after we arrived, I was taken into the clinic for another scan. I rolled my eyes at Christian. *Why are they bothering?* I thought. *It was bad enough the first time. This is just more heartache.*

Christian and I held hands as the sonographer once again rubbed jelly all over my belly and ran the scanner over the bump. She clicked a few buttons on her machine and the grainy picture came up on the screen. I looked away. I didn't need to see this.

'Mmmm . . .' she said, looking intently at the screen, clicking a few more buttons to 'zoom in' on the image.

'Well, it's there,' she said brightly.

'What? What's there?' I asked.

'The heartbeat.'

'What do you mean? Is my baby alive?'

'Yes. The heartbeat isn't as strong as I'd like, but it's definitely there.'

'Are you sure?' said Christian, incredulous.

'I'll bring the doctor in to confirm, but yes, I'm looking at the baby's heartbeat right now. See?' and she pointed at a little dark mass, pumping and pulsating. *Alive! My baby's alive!*

Tears sprang to my eyes. *Oh my god.*

When the doctor arrived he confirmed that the heartbeat was there and the baby was very much alive. *What if I'd taken the medicine? That would have killed my baby.* It was all too much to take in.

Christian was fuming.

'Why have we been told that the baby was dead?' he asked. 'I mean, we were here to have a removal. She was going to take the abortion pill – on your instructions!'

'The baby's heart is weak, which is probably why it was missed at your last scan,' the doctor explained. 'And as I understand from your notes, Miss Brooke, you suffered from *patent ductus arteriosus* as a child, which we know to be hereditary, so it is possible that this baby has similar issues. That is why we need to monitor you carefully. We consider this a high-risk pregnancy.'

'So what happens now?' asked Christian, looking as bewildered as I felt.

'I suggest you go home, rest and make another appointment to come back in six weeks' time. In the meantime, we'll refer you on to Great Ormond Street.'

I couldn't believe it. I was pregnant again.

The two of us went home in a daze. I didn't know whether to feel elated or furious. In truth, I felt both, as well as tremendous guilt that I had come within moments of terminating the life of my child – and all because of the stupid scan. They hadn't admitted they'd done anything wrong, of course. They were careful to cover themselves, even blaming the baby's weak heart for their failure to pick up the heartbeat in the first scan. But it really messed with my head and my feelings. In an instant, it seemed, everything changed. From now on, all I wanted was to protect this child growing inside me. I was meant to go back to work the following day but I was too distraught and called in sick. The whole experience had been so traumatic.

Although I had let my guvnor know I was pregnant, I

made a vow now that I wouldn't take any unnecessary risks. It was a totally different feeling to the one I'd had before the scare. Up until this moment I'd taken it for granted that being pregnant wouldn't change my attitude to work. After all, I always prioritized my job – only the car crash when I was pregnant with Amelia had made me take a step back. Now, this baby was what mattered most to me, and I decided that whatever happened next I wouldn't make any choices that could potentially put the baby's health in jeopardy. It wasn't just the fact that they supposedly had a weak heart – it was that I had spent two full days thinking I had lost them and wondering if it was my fault. Now I knew how hard it was to live with the thought of losing my baby, I resolved to ensure I made every decision in their best interest. For the next few weeks, I did very little covert work unless it was making phone calls or video calls. I focused instead on my Misper unit work. Unfortunately, sitting at my workstation for eight hours at a time, I started to suffer from back pain – an old, recurring injury that had been caused by a slipped disk years earlier, gained in the line of duty back in my Tower Hamlets days. Funnily enough, it was all down to Mo Habidi.

I'd just come out of Shadwell DLR station and was walking towards our offices when I spotted Mo disappearing into one of the bin stores at the bottom of a block of flats in Shadwell Gardens. *What the hell are you up to?* I wondered. He looked so shifty. So I followed him and knocked on the door. Since I was in plain clothes that day I didn't alert him to the fact that I was a copper so he simply swung the door open to let me in.

'Oh my god!' I exclaimed as I walked in to see five people all smoking crack. At that moment they realized I was a cop and the whole place started to shake as they fought to get out of the room. I made a grab for Mo – he was my nemesis and the one I wanted to catch – and at the same time, I pressed my radio and shouted: 'SHADWELL GARDENS! SHADWELL GARDENS!'

The team all knew that if I called for urgent assistance, I really meant it. I had hold of Mo but he was fighting to get away and we were scrapping for a while before I felt a huge weight on my back as some guy jumped on top of me from behind. My legs buckled and I collapsed, face down on the ground. But I kept hold of Mo and in that moment I felt a crack up my spine. Something had happened to my back. The other officers arrived soon after and I hobbled back to the station on tiptoes, feeling every single step up my spine. The chiropractor diagnosed a slipped disk and I was prescribed a course of anti-inflammatories. I had to spend the next few days lying on a wooden board to recover.

With my old injury playing up, I took a few days off from the Misper unit to rest my back, and was surprised when the sergeant in charge called me at home, three days into my sick leave.

'How you doing, Danni?' he asked, an edgy, impatient note to his voice.

'Not good,' I said. 'My back is killing me at the moment.'

'When are you coming back in?'

'I don't know . . . the doctor said he's happy to sign me off for a bit longer.'

'Mmmm . . . we're pretty short-staffed at the moment. Any chance you can come back in? Maybe shuffle some paperclips around?'

'What? No! I'm off with my back.'

'Well, at least can you give me an indication of when you'll be back?

'No, I can't.'

'Righto,' he let out a sigh. 'Okay, well, hope it gets better soon. Keep us updated, will you?'

And with that he hung up. *Bloody cheek!* I knew loads of people who went off sick for months and I'd hardly taken a day's sick leave in all the years I'd worked. Why was he picking on me? I'd dug out so much over the years, always putting the job first, working whenever they'd asked me, taking the shifts no one wanted. And yet, when I needed time off, there was no support whatsoever.

Shuffle paperclips? His words went round and round in my head. *Shuffle paperclips?* It was so denigrating to my work. I wasn't there to take up space. How could they have so little respect or compassion? These 'check-ins' were repeated over the next few days. In a fury, I rang my Police Federation rep and told them all about the phone calls. The Police Federation is the official union for the police force, and we had a detailed discussion on the phone where I described the situation in full as well as the details of my high-risk pregnancy.

'It's not fair,' I said. 'They are putting me under undue stress at a time I really don't need it. They're calling me every few days, putting pressure on me. Is that right? Do I have to put up with it?'

The federation convened a meeting with the management team and we confronted the sergeant who had been hassling me. He was unabashed.

'I thought maybe she could come in and do some light duties,' he shrugged.

'Like what?' said my rep coldly. 'Which light duties are you referring to? You mentioned these paperclips?'

'No!' he blustered. 'I didn't mean *actual* paperclips. That was just a figure of speech.'

'I see. But you didn't give an alternative. What other alternatives are there?'

'She could work in the front office.'

'That's a public-facing role. I'm sure you're well aware that pregnant colleagues are not allowed to deal directly with members of the public.'

An embarrassed silence filled the room. It was clear the sergeant had shot himself in the foot. He really didn't know what he was doing. He had been promoted in very quick time through the Met's acceleration programme and people like him made the worst police officers because they had no experience, no skills and no understanding of the work. Now my rep laid out in clear terms that I would be taking as long as I needed off work and I wasn't to be contacted at all in that time. If they absolutely had to get in touch it had to be by email only, but strictly no phone calls.

'She'll let you know when she's ready to come back,' he concluded. And that was that – I took the rest of the pregnancy off work.

If I'm being totally honest here, I probably wouldn't have

done that if it hadn't been for this sergeant and the way he treated me. I felt so insulted by his demeaning attitude I decided to stop trying to please everyone. For years I'd given my life to the police force, bending over backwards to accommodate everyone, working all the Christmas and holiday shifts, working overtime whenever I was asked, putting my life and health on the line when it was needed. Now I needed some compassion – how dare they treat me like some space filling desk jockey? I decided it was time I looked after myself and my unborn child.

So I stopped work and filled my time with therapeutic, relaxing activities, signing up for a floristry course during my pregnancy. My cousin Rachel, the paramedic, had seen the ad for the council-run course and because we both enjoyed doing things with our hands, we signed up at the same time. Once a week in a quiet village hall, we went along to our course and learned how to make all different types of floral arrangements, from hand-ties to wedding bouquets to funeral flowers. They taught us all the different techniques and the general principles of flower displays. We were the youngest there by a very long way, but I really liked it and when I took my flowers home at the end my mum was full of praise. 'They're really good, Danielle. Do me one next week, will you?'

It was totally out of my comfort zone but just what I needed – a slower, more relaxing pace of life. No pressure, no stress, everyone just chatting and arranging flowers. I liked it so much, in fact, that I took another course in Loughton, Essex to learn more about the technical side of arrangement.

I was so enthused about my new hobby that I even set up my own small floristry business in a disused toilet block in Wapping. Nobody had used the block for years but I realized that it was the perfect temperature for storing flowers, so Christian and I came to a reasonable arrangement with the site manager, cleaned it out, spruced it up and named our business 'Modicum of Decorum'. I loved it! It was such a nice little business, and I even got to meet a famous celebrity – Louis Theroux – who was buying flowers for his wife. I fan-girl'd hard, telling him how much I loved his shows, a world away from buying crack. I marvelled at how my colleagues probably wouldn't recognize me now. I'd gone from buying crack to selling chrysanthemums in the space of a few months!

During this time, I had a few appointments at Great Ormond Street, where monitoring showed we were expecting a boy and the heart condition cleared up on its own. At the same time, Christian was becoming increasingly unhappy in his work. I didn't know the full extent of it at the time because he kept a lot of it hidden, but the job he had been working was really tough. It was a paedophile case where he had to pose as a paedophile himself to get the suspect to admit his crimes. That was horrible, and I think by then he'd had enough. He never said explicitly that he wanted to leave the force but quietly he started putting out feelers for other jobs. After years of being someone else, I think he was ready to live in his own life for a while. Eventually, he was offered a job in the Netherlands investigating fraud for Nike. It was way more money than he was earning in the Met, with a lot less stress. The world of loss prevention was full of ex-coppers, and in this job his language skills would be put to good use, because a lot of the knock-offs were made in Morocco. We talked it through but, in the end, it was a no-brainer. He had to take the opportunity. We could visit him there, he could come home at weekends and between us I knew we would make it work.

In May 2011, Albert was born a week past his due date – a terrible, traumatic birth for us both. All the way along they had warned me that Albert was 'massive' but for some reason they still let me go past my due date. When my waters finally broke, I went to hospital and begged for an epidural, only to be told it was too soon, and then too late, to get one. Instead, someone tried unhelpfully to feed me a sandwich.

'I don't want a bloody sandwich, I want pain relief!' I yelled. Eventually, I started bearing down but something was wrong. The midwife hit the button above the bed and the room filled with doctors.

'What's happening?'

'We need to take you straight to theatre. This baby's stuck and is becoming distressed.'

They prepped me for surgery and took me down to theatre where I begged to try to push one last time. Now I gave it everything I had while the doctor grabbed the baby's head with forceps and tugged – once, twice and on the third pull he came out. The room was silent. No crying.

'Is he okay? Is my baby okay?' I wept, my legs in stirrups. I couldn't move to see what was happening. I'd been in some pretty terrible situations but this was the most vulnerable I'd felt in my entire life. Eventually, I heard a hiccupy little cry and the whole room breathed out in relief.

'He's a healthy ten pounds,' said the midwife. And that's when I went into shock.

My body started shaking and I passed out. When I woke up in the recovery room some moments later, I was lying next to my little boy, his face all bruised and scratched from the difficult birth.

'Oh no,' I started to cry. 'Is he okay? Oh, poor little boy!'

'He's going to be fine,' soothed the nurse. 'It looks worse than it is. It'll all be gone in a couple of days.'

She was right – although Albert looked like he'd gone five rounds with Tyson Fury he soon recovered, and I was just relieved that he was here in one piece. He was massive, so big in fact that he looked like a little Russian gangster baby. Nothing would satisfy him. I wanted to breastfeed him but I just couldn't get enough milk to hold him for long, so I quickly moved to bottles. Even then he woke frequently in the night, seemingly starving, and I wondered whether it might be an idea to give him solids early. The visiting midwife disagreed, saying he was far too young, but my mum supported me.

'You know your child best,' she said. 'Do what feels right for you.'

So we put him onto baby rice. It was the best decision we ever made. From that point onwards he slept better and was generally a healthier, happier baby.

Six weeks after the birth I took Albert and Amelia over to

the Netherlands for the summer holidays. I wanted to take the full year of maternity leave this time. Deep down I knew I wouldn't be having any more children, so I wanted to make the most of these precious early months, especially as I had missed out on spending this time with Amelia. The Netherlands was so cool – we all loved it. We hung out at the Nike offices, which were very modern and well-adapted to the needs of new parents. The offices all sat around a big green space with a running track on the outside and there was a bar on site, a holiday club for kids, a Starbucks, discount Nike shop and full Wi-Fi coverage for the whole space, so they were happy for people to sit with their laptops in the garden and work there. On Friday nights everyone went to the bar and mingled. I liked to go to the garden and hang out there, where I made friends with another lady who was taking her baby to work with her every day while she was breastfeeding. It was a revelation. This was a much more progressive working environment to the one I was used to. It seemed there were more adaptive ways of accommodating new mothers or fathers at work than simply sending them away for months at a time, and I found the whole atmosphere very friendly and welcoming.

All in all, it was a fabulous summer, and I only felt a small pang of guilt when I saw the London riots on TV and realized I was not there to help my colleagues. But I was enjoying my own life, for a change. Girls from Dagenham generally don't get to go to the Netherlands for weeks at a time; we spend two weeks in Spain each summer and that is it. Now I was enjoying a new world, going to the canal side every day, having lunch, visiting the lakes, popping over to Germany for the day and generally exploring with Christian and the kids. We had brought in a woman to run the flower shop for a while but in the end it became too much of a headache trying to manage it remotely, so we let her go. It had been a good little business, but I never saw it as anything more than a hobby. Besides, Christian was on a good salary and I still had my maternity pay. By September, I was back in the UK for Amelia to return to school and over the next six months we all spent a lot of time travelling back and forth to the Netherlands, exploring northern Europe. It was a wonderful, adventurous period for us all, though by spring 2012 it was nearly time for me to go back to work. Between the sick leave and the maternity leave, I had been off for nearly eighteen months. I'd loved every minute and felt my eyes had been opened to a completely different way of life. But it was time to get back to doing what I loved best – police work!

16

Break

'Hey, what's up?' Christian caught sight of my dejected look as I packed up the last of the kids' clothes into our overnight cases. We'd spent another wonderful weekend in the Netherlands with Christian but it seemed the time sped by. All too soon it was Sunday afternoon and I had to get everything in the car to catch the ferry back with Amelia and Albert.

'Nothing. I've just got that horrible feeling again,' I said. 'I don't want to go back. I want to stay here with you and the kids.'

'I want you to stay too,' he smiled. 'But you've got a job and Amelia has school.'

'I know . . . I know . . .' I muttered. My return to work hadn't gone exactly the way I thought it would. Though I was only working part-time to ease myself in, I hated it. I hated every part of it. It came as a shock. I'd always loved police work but something inside had shifted and now I resented being pulled away from the kids from 8 a.m. till 4 p.m. every single day. It was strange, because I'd spent all my adult life in a disciplined service so I knew that this was the commitment I'd made. I just didn't want to do it any more. I wanted to take Amelia to school every morning and be there for her at the school gates at home time. I didn't want to drop Albert in a nursery or leave him with family members. In the last eighteen months, both kids had got used to my being there all the time – and so had I. And I loved it. I loved being with them, getting to know them better, bonding as family. It felt like we were all spinning out into our separate orbits and I feared we were losing the closeness we'd shared.

Now that I was back in work I had to rely on other people again, accepting help from Christian's mum as well as my parents to manage my schedule, but each time I had to leave Albert with someone else I felt a jolt of anger. *Why do I have to hand over my child to look after other people's problems?* I was no longer in the Misper unit – since I'd been out of the job too long – so I'd been assigned a desk job in one of the borough's intelligence bureaus. It was boring as hell. I hoped that this was just a temporary feeling, an initial resistance to returning to the force after spending so long doing my own thing. But it didn't improve over time – in fact, it got worse. I just wasn't the same person. Now, I lived for the weekends when we either went to visit Christian in the Netherlands or he came to the UK. Every Friday afternoon I'd fly out the office door, collect Amelia from school, grab Albert and we'd hop onto the train or take the ferry. The train was quicker but I liked the ferry for the playrooms. It was only when Sunday night rolled around and I contemplated going back to the office the next day that the blues set in. And this feeling became harder and harder to bear.

My unhappiness didn't go unnoticed. But now the management team had changed and I had a really nice female superintendent called Diane. Some of the other officers gave Diane a hard time because she was upfront and blunt. She always got straight to the point and that rubbed some people up the wrong way, but I liked her because she had been a PC first, then a sergeant, working her way up through the ranks so she understood the job inside and out. Not like some of these young, arrogant types who had joined the force through the accelerated programme and were parachuted into management positions with little or no real experience. Diane and I talked quite openly with one another and one Monday morning, when she found me slumped over my desk in a funk, she observed: 'You're not happy here, are you?'

'No,' I sighed. 'I hate it. I hate this borough.'

'I don't like the borough either,' she admitted.

Tower Hamlets had been a great borough to work on because it was so busy and diverse. Every shift was different. But Waltham Forest was slow, quiet and unambitious. The most excitement we could expect from the day was a bit of shoplifting or the odd lost wallet. No drama. I felt too that the nature of our police work was different. It seemed to me that we were often responding rather than preventing. There was just a general lack of drive to suss things out. I had been shielded from this when I was in the Misper unit, but now I was working with the teams day in, day out, I found the general lack of assertiveness a little depressing.

One night I was out with an experienced officer in a van, driving past the high street, when I caught the unmistakable whiff of heroin.

I turned to him: 'Can you smell that?'

'Smell what?'

'Someone's cooking up.'

'No they're not.'

'Yeah, they are.'

I stopped the van and got out, trying to follow the scent to its origins. I wandered along the busy high street, past groups of kids, mothers with prams and elderly folk, my nose leading me to a disused phone box. I pulled opened the door and there was a middle-aged man in a heavy overcoat cooking up.

'SHIT!' he blurted out. Just as I was about to nick him for possession of a class A drug, the other officer gave me a quick tap on the shoulder.

'Can I have this arrest?' he asked excitedly. 'I've never seen this before.'

'Yeah, sure,' I said, bemused. *Never seen anyone smoking heroin?* And he had never smelled it either, because he didn't recognize the smell.

'How long you been in service?' I asked the officer on the way back to the station.

'Six years,' he said.

'And in six years you've never come across heroin before?'

'Well, I've seen it. I've just never seen it being smoked,' he shrugged.

'And if I hadn't been with you today you might go the rest of your police career never knowing what it smelled like, so you could conceivably never really bump into it?'

'Yeah, I guess.' He didn't consider this odd, which I found even more bizarre, but I guess that was typical of attitudes in Waltham Forest. This certainly wasn't cutting-edge police work.

I had no ambitions to climb the management ladder, taking the detective or inspector's courses as many of my colleagues did, because I already had a wonderful career with SCD10 that was progressing well. I knew one day I would take the NUTAC course and fulfil my ambitions to become a Level One officer. But when I returned to covert work, I found that too was disappointing. One of my first UC jobs after coming back from maternity leave was a club job round the back of Oxford Circus. The briefing was ridiculously generic: 'We think there's a coke dealer in this club. Can you go in and see what you can find?'

By now I knew one thing for absolute certain: there was a coke dealer in *every* club in *every* town and city up and down the country. You didn't need to be a genius to walk into a club and score coke. So I went in, found the dealer and got the evidence. *What am I really achieving here?* I wondered afterwards. *As soon as this guy is off the streets another dealer will step in to take his place.* It was simple supply and demand. Anyone with half a brain could see this was a pretty pointless exercise. Even the prostitute jobs were dull and uninspiring. Standing round in Hackney in a red-light area waiting for punters, I tried to summon up some enthusiasm, but my heart just wasn't in it any more. It was the same all night long: the punter pulled over, told me what he wanted, I said no and made my excuses. Then he'd drive off and get nicked further up the road. I did this over and over again for hours at a time. It felt pointless and repetitive – were we really making anything safer for the girls on the street? Trudging home afterwards, I realized this kind of work no longer gave me the same buzz as before. It felt like a step backwards from the long-term UFO jobs I'd done, and unfulfilling.

Then something happened – Christian was headhunted by France's biggest sporting goods shop, Chausport, and offered a very well-paid role as a regional manager. It was closer to home, better pay and a good career move . . . and it gave me the incentive to think about our lives as a family, a whole unit. Why were we spending so much time apart? The togetherness we had created as a family during my maternity leave was slipping away. This was the perfect opportunity to bring us together again.

'Why don't I take a career break and move to France with you and the kids?' I suggested. 'I'm not happy being away from Amelia and Albert while they're so young. I can go back once they've grown up a bit. Plus, they'll have the opportunity to live abroad and learn French.'

He readily agreed. He missed having us all around and the house seemed too big and quiet with no one in it. Fortunately, Diane was on my side, and when I approached her she authorized a five-year career break, which was pretty amazing. I don't think you could get that now. The police offer career breaks because they recognize that their personnel want to pursue other interests for a time, expanding their skillset. I was offered five years off work, with a twenty-eight-day notice period to return.

Next, I had to convince Amelia's dad to let her come with

us. It wasn't easy – I had to prove to him that I would stick to our arrangements and regularly bring her back for their weekends together. I also had to convince him that it was an incredible opportunity for his eight-year-old daughter to attend a French school. It wasn't easy, but eventually he signed it off. My parents understood too – they knew how much I regretted not spending time with Amelia when she was very young and how keen I was to make up for lost time. My dad in particular was aware of just how much work I'd taken on while I was in SCD10 and that I probably needed the rest. My mum was sad she wouldn't see her grandkids every day, and she had a special bond with Amelia because she'd looked after her so much in her early years, but she was excited for me that I'd be at home a lot more. She used to say: 'You've had these children for me. I love them so much.' That really got my hackles up. Now, at last, I was going to be the one to take care of them instead of her.

The only ones who took it badly were my colleagues on the UC team.

'Are you sure?' asked John. 'Is this really what you want?'

'Yes, it is,' I said. 'I need to do this for me, for my kids.'

'You'll be bored as hell at home all the time.'

'I'll take that risk,' I smiled.

To be honest, I think they assumed I left because Christian had left too, but it had nothing to do with him. My priorities had changed and now I just wanted to be with my children.

We rented a four-bedroom house in Lille and began the difficult task of setting up our new lives together. It was hard for me, because my French didn't go much further than

A level, so I really had to work at understanding people and making myself understood. It was a big change for the kids too. On Amelia's first day at school she was so nervous she was physically shaking. I fretted about her all day long but when she came out she had a great big grin on her face and said everyone had been really kind to her. Within a couple of months she could recite a poem about a hedgehog in French, which made me so happy. I couldn't believe my daughter was growing up bilingual!

Secretly, I *was* a little worried that I might get bored at home. I'd laughed at John when he warned me this might happen but at the back of my mind, I shared the same concern. What if a life at home didn't suit me? What if I was sitting around all day long, bored out of my mind? So I set myself challenges; like teaching myself certain dishes I'd wanted to learn how to cook, learning about the area or finding clubs for the kids. Every day I'd pick up Amelia from school during their two-hour lunch break and took Albert for all sorts of fun activities, like visiting Lille Zoo, going swimming or exploring our local parks. The school week is different in France. They have Wednesday afternoons off and school on Saturday morning, so someone had to be around for all those school runs and I loved the fact that it was me. I got closer to the kids in all senses.

Prior to the move, we had no set routine with school because I was always running around, managing everything on the hoof. Now we could plan the week's activities without disruption, so Amelia took swimming lessons, dance classes and sports clubs. I had time to make the costumes for her school plays instead of buying something off the shelf and I could spend time with her at night and help her with her homework. We sat down to eat together, I was cooking again, making traditional Italian dishes from scratch and aromatic authentic curries. Those were Amelia's favourite. I did her hair nicely, spent time with Albert and just really enjoyed being Mum. In time, Amelia showed a real talent for running and we took her to track meets all over France. Lille is in the north, close to the border with Belgium and well connected to the rest of Europe, and we often took trips at the weekend, sometimes to the south of France and at other times to Switzerland. I discovered a real thirst for travel, enjoying going to new places and finding out about the people there. Meanwhile, Christian and I got on great. It was a very harmonious and stress-free period and I appreciated every minute.

The thing I found most difficult was that Christian now paid for all the household expenses. I had always paid my way before and I tried to contribute, but he wouldn't hear of it.

'You don't want to touch your savings,' he told me. 'It makes no difference in the end that the money is coming from my side of things, we're both contributing equally to this household. The only difference is my job is remunerated and yours isn't.'

He was right – it was a full-time position, being Mum. And don't get me wrong, I loved it. I just found it weird not to be spending my own money. Christian did his best to make me feel comfortable with the arrangement and I knew there was nothing I wanted to do that I couldn't do. The problem was entirely in my own head. I had always equated earning my own money with my freedom and it was a mental shift that took time to accept.

And it was just one tiny issue in comparison to the amazing lifestyle we now enjoyed. Christian was often required to travel to other parts of France for his job and we frequently accompanied him while he was on these trips. So while he went to the office, I'd take the kids to the beach. One time we had travelled to Nice and it occurred to me we were now just an hour from the border with Italy.

'Shall we have pizza for lunch in Italy?' I suggested to the kids.

'Yeah!' Amelia's eyes lit up. So we did. It was a joyful, free, exciting period and very quickly Amelia became fluent in French, which was wonderful. It was the complete opposite from my old life, a chance to create the happy, cohesive family unit I had always yearned for. And I was never, for one moment, bored.

The subject of marriage never came up between us. My first marriage had been a disaster so I had no desire to go back there again. And Christian came from a very laid-back, unconventional upbringing so neither of us were keen to get hitched. At some point he told me he was writing a book about his time in the force, his memoir. I didn't think much about it at first. I was so wrapped up in the kids and enjoying our lives together and it seemed wholly natural that Christian would turn his hand to writing. He was an extraordinarily clever person and it was obvious to me that he would be able to do something like that. A few months later, he asked if he could mention me and of course I agreed because I trusted him implicitly. The book soon attracted a publisher and when he handed me the manuscript I was fascinated to read about a host of his undercover stories that had made it into print. It wasn't all easy reading. The title was *Crossing the Line: Losing Your Mind as an Undercover Cop*, and it described how the pressures of the job got too much for him. I was disturbed to read just how near the edge he had been when he left. It was brave for him to open up like this and I told him so. Importantly, he didn't reveal any big secrets about our work or betray any confidences. Nevertheless, we got wind that the UC lot were unhappy, though I didn't think hard about this at first. It all felt so far away.

The book was published in May 2013, and a few months later we travelled to the Edinburgh Book Festival for a series of talks and book-signing events. We had dinner with his publishers and even managed to take in a couple of shows. Christian was now a published author and this was something I found very exciting. I'd never done 'the Fringe' before. It was so far removed from my world – to my mind that was only something yuppies did. In fact, if you asked my mum what the Edinburgh Fringe was, she'd probably tell you it was a haircut! It was all very glamorous, very cool and it was the first time that it all struck me as a little bit 'celebrity'.

Then, when we got home, the shit hit the fan. One night in our dining room in France I caught sight of Christian on the computer, hunched over, his head in his hands. 'What's up?' I asked. He wasn't a hugely demonstrative person, so it was strange to see him upset.

'They're really not happy about the book,' he said.

'Who?

'The UC unit. I could get into quite a lot of trouble about it.'

He seemed distressed but didn't want to show me what they had said so I assumed it would probably be all right in the end. After all, he was known as 'Golden Balls' back in the day, one of their brightest stars. Whatever was going on, I was sure it would blow over. But it didn't. Emails pinged back and forth, there was a lot of anger and noise, though Christian was careful not to tell me too much. Technically, I was still in service so he felt it wouldn't be right to draw me into his rows with the SCD10 lot. But I could see what was happening from afar and I guessed it had something to do with the wider context.

During this time, the Mark Kennedy story had broken. Mark Kennedy was a Level One covert officer who had been tasked with infiltrating environmental and left-wing protest groups. Mark had entered into several relationships with women involved in these protest groups – with the alleged knowledge of his superiors – and one had even had his baby. Now his cover was blown, these women were shocked at discovering his true identity and were suing the force for deception. It was a terrible situation, and I had every sympathy for the women involved – things should never have got that far – but the whole affair had brought down a lot of criticism on the Met and especially the covert unit.

The story sent shock waves through SCD10, and people started dropping like flies. John left and was replaced with someone who, as far as any of us were aware, had no experience being deployed undercover. Vic and Michael left too. There was a major shake-up at the unit which, thankfully, I didn't experience up close, because I was on the other side of the Channel. I know that this won't be a popular thing to say, but I had a lot of sympathy for Mark. I don't deny that he did a lot of things he shouldn't have, but he wasn't given any support or direction by his command and when the story broke he didn't get any help. He was forced to take the blame alone when he was acting on the direction of superior officers. The Met knew what he was doing all along – and he wasn't the only one – but they just washed their hands of him. I don't defend his actions. They were wrong and I can't imagine being one of the women he deceived, but he was sent in there and he acted with the full knowledge of his handlers. So, by the time Christian's book surfaced, the Met in general, and the covert unit in particular, were already under fire and in siege mode.

They overreacted, and that's when I got dragged in.

One morning a rather innocent-looking email landed in my inbox from someone who worked on the covert team.

`Hi - how are things?` it read. There was a little bit of small talk and then they posed the question: `Are you still with Christian?`

When I replied, 'yes', they responded: `Tell him he's not welcome back in London and if anyone sees him they're going to headbutt him.`

I was shocked. First, that anyone would even involve me in Christian's affairs, but second, that they would threaten a former well-respected and admired member of the team with physical violence. It was thuggish and thoroughly unpleasant.

Christian was furious. It was one of the only times I'd seen him really angry.

'How dare they drag you into it!' he said. 'We're two separate people. I can't believe they would resort to such stupid, playground threats.'

It wasn't much – just that one line: 'tell him he's not welcome back . . .' – but it changed everything for me.

The thought of returning to that unit now made me sick to my stomach. How could I go back and trust them with my life again? They had made threats to the father of my child. And if I didn't go back to covert work, I certainly wasn't going to consider returning to the force just to sit in the Waltham Forest intelligence unit. Technically, I still had four years left on my career break, but I wasn't allowed to work anywhere else during that time without permission from the force, and now it occurred to me that I might one day want to do other things. If I was still tied to the Met, I couldn't do that without their permission. And I didn't like that idea. I was young enough to start another career. God knows what that would be, but I knew I could learn other skills – my foray into floristry had taught me that. Now, for the first time, a thought formed in my mind: *What if I don't go back?*

When I told my dad I was thinking of leaving the force altogether he wasn't happy. He thought it was a big risk – and he wasn't one of life's risk-takers.

'Why not just see out your career break until you have a definite plan?' he suggested. 'Where is the harm in that?'

'I need to be free to make my own decisions, Dad,' I said. 'I don't know what I want yet. But I won't be able to consider other options while I'm still tied to the Met.'

'Hmmm . . . I still think it's a mistake but, well, it's your life, Danni.'

It wasn't a decision I took lightly, but in the end I went with my gut. Whatever the UC unit looked like now it certainly wasn't the same place I'd been welcomed into ten years earlier.

So at the end of 2013, after a decade in the police force, I wrote my resignation email. I never thought I would say this, but it was a relief when I finally pressed the send button. For so many years I had loved my job and always thought I was in the force for life, but after that threat I knew I could never return, so leaving was my only option. Weirdly, I didn't get a reply for months. Finally, when they bothered to 'accept' my resignation early in 2014, they insisted I hand back my warrant card. There was no 'we're sorry to see you go' or 'can we invite you for an exit interview?' Nothing like that. As it turned out, I didn't have my warrant card – HR had taken my card and cuffs and cleared my locker out when I left for my career break. Now I was free and could do what I wanted without restrictions. I could open a Facebook page, which I'd never done before, and was free to take work anywhere I wanted without permission. It was like taking a big jacket off. A weight was off my shoulders, and I decided to put that whole period of my life in a box, forget about it and enjoy my time in France.

For a working-class girl from a council estate in Dagenham,

I felt so incredibly lucky. People from my part of the world rarely got an opportunity to live abroad and explore other countries, customs and cultures, so I just soaked it all up. As a young girl I had harboured a crazy fantasy that I would grow up to marry a French doctor. It was a bit of a fangirl affair with the country, to be honest. I loved the accent, the fashion, the way they drank red wine, the way they did everything! The French all seemed so sophisticated and classy. Now I had the chance to live out my fantasy – albeit with a former copper, not a doctor – and my French improved too, thankfully. Paris was my favourite city in the world and I loved that I could explore Europe by just driving over borders.

Whatever happened next, I was ready to make my own decisions. I had been through so much already – personally and professionally – I now had confidence in my own resources and skills to take control. I had spent my entire working life being told what to do so it was at once liberating, scary, exciting and thrilling to take charge. For the first time in my adult life, I was truly free.

17

A New Direction

I was in the queue at the bank near my mum's house when I took the call from Nic, my old mate from SCD10.

'How you doing, Nic?' I was so thrilled to hear from her. She too had left the force and it had been ages since we'd had a proper catch up. I was in the UK with the kids for the weekend on one of my regular trips back, staying at my mum's place in Kent. On this occasion, I had arranged to meet my friends for dinner in Essex the following night.

'Hey Danni, I've got this job come up,' she said. 'It's in Camden. It's a good day rate – can you come along tomorrow?'

It looked like I had time to squeeze in the work and since I was now free to make my own career decisions I said yes, assuming that it was a private investigator (PI) engagement tracking down a missing person, the kind of PI job which I knew Nic had taken on before.

At midday the following day, I teetered along Gloucester Avenue in my heels, leather trousers, fur coat and the biggest blow dry you've ever seen in your life, as I was due to meet my Essex friends afterwards and I didn't often get the chance to get glammed up in France. But when I arrived at the address Nic had given me, I was confused. It was the glass-fronted office of a company called Shine TV. *What is this? Seems a bit weird to be meeting here.* Nevertheless, I went up to the receptionist and presented myself.

'Danni Brooke – I'm here to meet, er, someone,' I said to her with some uncertainty.

'Yes, of course,' she said. 'Lucy will be along in a moment. Please take a seat.'

The offices were plush, very modern and there were all sorts of young trendy things crossing back and forth. Soon, a petite, pretty lady called Lucy appeared. She was dressed in very cool clothes and she greeted me warmly and walked me through to a meeting room.

'Please come in,' she gestured for me to sit down. I followed her slowly, warily, my face a frown of incomprehension.

'Danni, do you know why you're here?' she asked.

'No. What is this?'

'You really don't know?'

'No.'

'Nic said you'd be really good at this.'

'Is this TV?' I asked.

'Yeah, it is.'

'Nope. I'm not doing that,' I said resolutely. I had spent my entire life under the radar. I wasn't going to expose myself now. I got up to leave.

'Please let me explain,' she said hurriedly. 'We're shooting a pilot for a new TV show called *Hunted*. Ordinary people go on the run and we have a team of former police, military and intelligence personnel tasked with tracking them down. It's a real-life, real-time investigation into the powers of the surveillance state in game form. If the contestants are successful and evade capture for twenty-eight days, they win a prize at the end.

'Nic is already on board and we have a number of other serving and former officers, as well as former MI5 agents. Nic tells us you've got the skills to join the team and, well, you're here now. Why not just do a little piece to camera?'

What the hell is a piece to camera?

'No, forget it. I'm not going on the telly,' I said again. 'Look, you seem really nice, Lucy. You really do, so I'm sorry to let you down, but I had no idea that's what I was coming here for and, well, I can't be on TV. I just can't.'

I was thinking of all the criminals I'd put away over the years, the people who had spent time in jail thanks to me, looking up at the TV screen and seeing my mug on there. Many still had no idea I was a copper. Being exposed on TV could affect mine and my family's safety. It was simply too risky.

Lucy tried again.

'Well, Nic explained the line of work you were in together and, since this is only a screen test, there's no guarantee it will necessarily make it onto TV. We take it round the TV channels as a way to show them what we'd like to make. Then we make a pilot and on the back of that they will decide to commission a series or not. It's not actually going to be on the telly yet.'

'Do you guarantee this won't be on TV?'

'Absolutely. I guarantee this is not going to be on telly. Anything we film here today is purely for commissioning editors, not for the public. The pilot might not even get commissioned so you may never hear from me again.'

She was very persuasive, this Lucy, and I didn't want to keep saying no, so in the end I buckled, which annoyed me.

The funny thing was, the moment she turned the camera on, I started 'performing'. I have no idea where it came from or why I did it, but I felt like someone flicked a switch and I was now acting a part – the bubbly, expressive, engaging Danni. TV Danni! It had been exactly the same with my covert work where, unconsciously, I'd slip on a mask, immersing myself in another persona for a while. Lucy sat next to the camera, prompting me with questions, and without having to be told, I incorporated her questions into my answers so it seemed like I was giving a spontaneous monologue. When we paused for a break Lucy said: 'You're doing great. I can't believe you've never done this before. I don't even have to give you direction on technique.'

I smiled at the compliment. She was so nice! *Is everyone in TV as nice as her?* I wondered. I was used to banter and piss-taking, not flattery. This felt to me like play-acting, the same kind of stuff I'd been doing undercover all those years. I was still me, just an exaggerated version of myself, and to be honest, it came naturally. By the time I exited the building onto the busy streets of Camden I felt slightly bewildered but also pretty certain that it had gone well.

The following week I got a phone call from Lucy: 'Are you free in two weeks? They've commissioned the pilot and we want you on the team.'

Lucy gave me all the details, and once I put the phone

down I sat back and had a think. I recalled my teenage self, indulging in the same dreams as other girls my age, longing to be 'a famous star on TV'. But by the time I reached sixteen I felt it was too late. *I've missed my chance to be famous*, I told myself. Now someone was inviting me to be on the telly at the grand old age of thirty-odd. I wondered what my teen self would make of that! Was this a golden opportunity I couldn't afford to pass up or a silly fantasy, one which could potentially harm me and my family? That night I sat down with Christian and we talked it all through. He himself had 'broken cover' with his book, which was well received by the public, and he said he didn't have any regrets about 'outing' himself.

'Besides, you're not baring your soul to the world,' he said. 'It's a show. Do you want to do it?'

'Yeah, I do.'

'So, what's holding you back? We can protect our family life. Nobody has to know where you live. It's an opportunity and maybe if you don't do it you'll regret it.'

I appreciated Christian's support. It meant a lot to have him on my side and since I didn't have a career right now I knew that it was important to start exploring options. This had landed in my lap and I'd be crazy not to give it a go. Fortunately, the pilot was successful and it wasn't long afterwards that we were asked to return to shoot for the first series. The next hurdle was working out the logistics. Filming would take me away from the kids for weeks at a time and since Christian was working it looked like I might have to fall back on my mum again to help out. Christian and I were discussing all of this one night in France, both coming to the slow realization that I might actually have to relocate to Kent for a while, when something struck me. Though we were still the best of friends, Christian and I no longer shared romantic feelings for each other. I couldn't remember the last time we had kissed. It wasn't as if either of us had noticed either. It just seemed to have fizzled out quietly, without fanfare.

'This . . .' I pointed at him and then me. 'Us. It's not working any more, is it?'

'I don't think so,' he said slowly. There was no big drama, no tears even. Neither of us were living in misery, it just felt like our relationship had settled in its natural place, which was friendship.

'Is that okay?' I said, recalling the years of trauma I'd been through with Tom.

'It's okay,' he said. And, as if reading my mind, he took my hand in his and looked at me seriously.

'Danni, honestly. It's okay. We are still a team. We will *always* be a team. Nothing is going to change that so don't worry. You're the mother of my son. I'm on your side.'

It was strange and a little sad to let go of each other, but not scary. I knew Christian and I would be friends for life. There would be no animosity, no difficulties with arrangements, no drama. Christian had seen everything I had been through with Tom, he had witnessed it first hand, and I knew he would never put me through that.

So, early in 2014, I packed our suitcases and took the kids to my mum's place in Kent. She had generously agreed to look after them while I was away on location with Shine filming for four weeks, and Christian was due to come and spend time with them all at weekends. I had loved my time in France but I hadn't planned on being a French homemaker forever and I needed to move forward with my life. Christian was still living and working in France and we would always be in touch because of Albert. We had been there for each other during a very important part of our lives and drawn strength from the partnership we created as we each, separately, left the force. My eighteen months in France had been very healing, a chance to recalibrate, to find out what I wanted and to set in place some new habits and routines for us all as a family. But now I was heading in a new direction. We told the kids that work commitments meant we were living apart so there was no big 'separation'. They took their cue from us and just carried on without drama.

Early one morning, I was picked up by car and whisked off to grand old Bromley to be briefed for the show. There, we were shown pictures of the fugitives and given intelligence on them, including their last known locations, fed from the intel team. The best thing was that Nic and I had been paired together as a 'hunting' team so it was like the old days again. We were given the basic outline of what would happen. The fugitives would go on the run and a central London team, led by former copper Bret Lovegrove, would attempt to track them through surveillance. Bret was a huge man but seemed very friendly. His deputy was former detective Peter Bleksley, whom everyone called Bleks. I'd heard of Bleks before – he was notorious in the covert world, a bit of a legend. The HQ team fed the teams of 'hunters' on the ground crucial intelligence to allow us to follow and then catch the fugitives. There would be a camera crew with us at all times, and one with the fugitives too, so the viewer could experience the drama from the point of view of both the hunters and the hunted. From the start I felt comfortable with the set-up and the people. It was like being a cop on the ground while the HQ team acted as our intelligence unit. All the hunters and trackers were former cops, intelligence and service personnel so we all spoke a common language. The only ones who seemed a little alien were the super-friendly TV people. They were all very much like Lucy, incredibly 'nice' and smiley, telling you how wonderful you were, even as they asked you to reshoot something you'd already done fifteen times!

It didn't get off to the best start. Our first fugitives were a wife and wife team and when we captured them on day two, one half of the couple reacted so badly she actually went for Nic. It was all caught on camera. We tracked them down in the middle of a busy high street and when we apprehended them, this woman became very aggressive and tried to fight us off. Nic wasn't happy.

'I didn't sign up for this,' she said in her hotel room that night. 'I took a lot of aggro when I was in the police but this isn't real. This is just telly. If people think they can attack us for what we're doing then I'm getting out.'

'They can't all be like her,' I reasoned. This particular woman took it all far too seriously. Driving her back to the van after her capture she kept leaning over to say nasty things to me. *Is she doing this for the camera or is she an arsehole for real?* Either way, I wasn't going to put up with it. So every time she leaned towards me I braked hard and she got a jolt.

'Why don't you just calm down?' I suggested. 'There's no need to get this wound up.'

That night they put us all in the same hotel, which was a big mistake. Our narky fugitive drank too much white wine and started shouting at us, telling us how much better than us she was and that we shouldn't have caught her first. She was probably just annoyed and embarrassed at getting caught so quickly but it felt so stupid. This was a bloody TV show, not real life. We both left and went back up to the room.

'She should never have been allowed on this show,' I said as Nic packed up her things.

'Her wife seems really nice, and actually a bit embarrassed by her behaviour, but you'd think they would screen people better. The next lot won't be so bad, I reckon.'

'Personally, I don't care,' she said. 'If that's what they think is acceptable on day two, I hate to think what it's going to be like when we capture someone on day twenty. It's not worth it, Danni. I'm getting out.'

Nic was adamant she was walking and she told our contact on Shine TV that night, at which point I got a call from one of the production executives, begging for my help.

'What can I do to keep her?' he said. 'Please talk her round.'

'I don't know what to tell you,' I said. 'This was not what either of us were expecting. She says it's not worth the money.'

They had bought us champagne that night, supposedly for the 'first capture', but I knew it was really to butter us up. They may have got some dramatic footage but Nic had taken the brunt of some very unpleasant behaviour and they could see we weren't impressed.

'Do you think she wants more?' he asked. 'We can work with her on that. Find out how much money she wants.'

So I went back to Nic's room.

'They really want you to stay and they're offering you more money. He's asked how much you want.'

We were very green. At this point we had no idea how TV worked and that once you started filming you couldn't just swap people in and out. It would be bad for continuity. That ignorance played to our advantage.

'How much do you think I can get?' Nic looked at me.

'I don't know but if you're getting it I want it too.'

So we agreed a 50 per cent increase of our day rate.

'She will stay but she wants more money and obviously if she's getting paid more I want the same,' I said when I rang the TV executive back. I told them the figure and they agreed straight away. *Damn, should have asked for more!*

I called Nic: 'They said yes.'

'Great – see you in the morning!'

The rest of the captures were pretty uneventful and after a month on location, it was over. I hadn't liked living out of a suitcase for weeks at a time, and I had missed the kids like crazy, but the whole experience was very enjoyable, like a giant, grown-up game of hide and seek. And I got to do it with Nic, which made it even sweeter. Best of all, I could go home and be a full-time mum again. One fugitive we hunted was a police officer, who obviously knew the pitfalls to avoid and remained on the run for a couple of weeks. This felt like a proper challenge and Nic and I both agreed we really wanted to get him. He had been quite successful at first, hiring a Winnebago and taking himself deep into the mountains. At one point our intelligence led us to the base of a mountain in Devon and the producers told us we needed to climb up it. But that came from the producer, not the intelligence team. I'm not a climber so I had no interest in going up the mountain and I put my foot down. It was obvious they were trying to create a 'scene' for TV.

'There's no intelligence to put us up there,' I said firmly. 'So no, I'm not going up that mountain. It will just make us look stupid.'

A little while later, while driving on the road beyond the mountain we took a wrong turning and arrived at a dead end. We spun the car around, started driving back and let a Winnebago pass in front of us. I looked at the driver.

'That's him!' I shouted. Our fugitive was driving the Winnebago! We turned the car around and started to chase. The cameraman beside me was giddy as a kipper – he couldn't believe his luck.

'Remember, if it's not on camera it didn't happen', was the little phrase he liked to use to remind us that everything we did needed to be captured on film. Now he was breathless with excitement that he was actually filming a real-life chase. We sped along for a short while until we were stopped by a farmer walking his cows in the road. The Winnebago braked and the door flew upon. He started to run. This guy was six two and could easily outpace us both – Nic was even shorter than me! He started running across a field and when he got to the other side, he jumped over a barbed wire fence into a stream. I jumped after him and landed face down in the stream. I was soaking wet but, still, I refused to give up and we found him in the end, hiding behind a tree, where I delivered the lines: 'Your time on the run is over. You've been hunted.' My capture. It was always my capture!

Back in the real world, we moved into Mum's place while I searched for a house nearby to rent. The kids didn't mind – they loved staying with their nana and grandad, where they each had a room of their own and were indulged with the sort of crap, processed food I refused to serve them. Since Nic and I had got so many captures we were selected to do lots of the press interviews for the TV launch, with Peter Bleksley and a former intelligence officer who worked alongside him called Ben Owen.

Channel 4 had selected the four of us to be the 'face' of *Hunted*. We were given media training, shot some promos and were paraded around the press and TV studios to 'sell' the series to the public. I found it all rather exhilarating. This was a world away from the one I was used to. I'd spent years standing around on street corners, buying drugs. Now I was whisked from one studio to the next in taxis, everyone falling over themselves to meet my every whim. At times I even found it a little embarrassing.

'No, it's okay,' I told one lovely runner. 'I can get my own water.'

And I'm just a nobody! I thought. *Imagine how they'd treat me if I was an actual star.* No wonder so many celebrities ended up like spoiled divas. If you experienced this kind of pampering 24/7, it would be so easy to start to expect the five-star treatment wherever you went.

I realized this wasn't prime-time TV and we weren't going to be megastars, but the first time I opened *Grazia* magazine and saw my own face staring back at me from the pages of an article titled 'The Real Life 21 Jump Street', I was beside myself with excitement. The only downside was that I was dressed in a leather jacket with my hair scraped back in a high ponytail, wearing my best 'moody bitch' face.

'Bloody hell!' I exclaimed to my mum. 'All these years I've been reading this magazine with all these fabulous girls in it and now I'm in it myself and I look like that!'

I pointed at the picture.

'I think you look nice,' she said, reading over my shoulder.

'Mum, you always say that! I didn't want to look nice, I wanted to look glamorous.'

'It says here you worked undercover . . .'

'Oh, er . . . yeah.'

'What's that about then?'

Shit.

18

Mr and Mrs Smith

'Well, I worked undercover in order to infiltrate various criminal networks . . .' I started.

'The same as Christian?' My stepdad had read Christian's book so they both knew about his work as a covert officer.

'Yes, the same as Christian.'

'Buying drugs and guns and things from gangs?' Mum asked.

'Yes.'

'From gangs? Buying drugs from gangs?' she repeated, her voice rising a few octaves.

'Yeah.'

'Undercover? So not in your uniform then?'

'No.'

'Why didn't you tell me that? Why have I got to read it in the magazine before you'll tell your own mother?'

'Well, it wasn't *everything* that I did,' I said weakly.

'And it's so dangerous!' she went on. 'Why would you do that? What do you want to be doing putting yourself in danger like that? You should have let the others do it.'

This is precisely why I didn't tell you, I thought.

'It's just irresponsible,' she was muttering, more to herself than to me. 'You don't need to do that, running around with gangs. A mother of two children! What if they hurt you?'

'Mum, I don't do it any more. I left the police. Remember?'

This was exactly the response I had imagined from my mum – protective and disapproving – which is why I had never told her at the time. Why give her unnecessary worry? But I did feel bad that I hadn't told her about my secret life before speaking to the press about it. She should have known first. Everything had just moved so quickly, like a juggernaut, and before I knew it adverts for the show were plastered all over the sides of buses and telephone boxes in the build-up to the launch.

In September 2015, the first episode aired and I watched it in my mum's living room with a bottle of champagne. Seeing how they edited all the clips together it was quite a gripping hour of television and, even though it was a bit cringey to see myself up there on TV, the show was put together so well none of us stood out individually. Mum was really happy – to her mind this was a big step up in the world and she was very proud of me. The first series was popular with the public too, pulling in around 2 million viewers a week, which was apparently very good for Channel 4, so they recommissioned it and we were all rehired. In November 2015, we were invited to a swanky TV bash by Channel 4 called 'The Upfronts' which had something to do with selling advertising. Now here was an opportunity to get really glammed up!

*

'Oh my god, it's Tony from *Hollyoaks*!' I squealed to Nic. I was so excited I could hardly contain myself. We were in the green room, as we had been asked to present an award and give a short speech about the show, and now we watched as all the famous faces from Channel 4 made their entrances.

'Oh my god, it's Jon Snow!' I nudged Nic. I was so starstruck.

Then: 'It's the guys from *Tattoo Fixers*!'

Moments later: 'Kirsty and Phil. Nic, It's Kirsty and Phil!'

I'd been watching *Location, Location, Location* all my life. I'd grown up seeing these people and now we were actually in the room together, it was unbelievable. I had this very weird sense that I *knew* them all, but of course I didn't, and they knew nothing about me. They all looked super relaxed, as if they'd done this a hundred times before, whereas everything was new to me.

'Yeah, yeah . . .' Nic said. By now she was fed up with my frequent 'alerts' as to who had just arrived at the bash.

After a few drinks I headed into the unisex toilets. *Unisex*, I marvelled, *very modern, very cool*. I unzipped my jumpsuit, but since the long zip was at the back I needed help to do it back up. I had assumed that when I came out there would be another woman there I could ask for help. Instead, when I came out, the only person I saw was Sketch, one of the male stars of *Tattoo Fixers*. *Well, I can't very well leave with my jumpsuit undone . . .*

'Excuse me, mate,' I said sheepishly. 'I don't suppose you can do me up at the back, please?'

'Yeah, sure,' he said. So I leaned over the sink and he got

hold of the zipper behind me. Just then a woman wandered into the loos and, seeing us in that position, exclaimed: 'Oh, I'm really sorry!' and, startled, she backed out again.

'Oh no, it's not what you think!' I said quickly. 'He's doing up my jumpsuit!'

It was like a scene from a *Carry On* film. After she left Sketch and I looked at each other and fell about laughing.

It was such a funny and strange night all in all. I spent a lot of time chatting to Ben, the ex-British intelligence officer who worked with Bleks in our *Hunted* 'intelligence' HQ. He also found the entertainment world a little alien, having come up through the ranks of the military and then leading intelligence teams in counterterrorism and espionage. He had some fascinating stories to tell and, far from making friends with the new telly people, I ended up talking to Ben all night. At the end of the evening I went to say goodbye and he went in for a kiss. And I kissed him back. I was in utter shock. I wasn't expecting it. He then walked me to my waiting car. He was very good-looking but I had no idea he even liked me and that night, when I went home, I was mortified. I had vowed to myself I wouldn't get involved with anyone at work again and yet here I was, snogging the guy from the office! The next day was Amelia's birthday, and as well as having the hangover from hell I was also really upset at what I'd done. So when he messaged me on Telegram: How's the head? I replied very bluntly fine, then didn't hear from him at all until Christmas Day, when he texted: Happy Christmas!

It was all a bit confusing, to be honest. I liked him but I worried about getting involved with someone on the programme. What if it all went tits up and we still had to work together? I knew how difficult that could be after my time with Tom. Besides, I felt that if he was interested he would have called by now, asking to meet up. So I put him out of my mind. Then, in February 2016, we bumped into one another at Channel 4 and afterwards he walked me to the tube. It was all very cordial, very friendly, but he didn't mention anything about us so I assumed that our party kiss had just been a one-off, drunken snog. *Forget about it, Danni. He's not interested.*

We started filming again in April for the second series and Ben and I stayed in touch during the filming schedule. One night, he sent me a message saying he hoped to see me in London. So when me and Nic were deployed to the capital, a few of us went for drinks after filming. That night Ben declared his undying love and the rest, as they say, is history! I had liked him all along but I didn't think he thought of me that way – meanwhile, he thought I was playing hard to get. I suspect our colleagues had spotted the spark and had done a bit of manoeuvring to get me down to London for the drinks. Once we were an item, it felt so natural and right. I loved spending time with Ben, hearing about his career and what he had achieved. It was all so impressive. We would stay up for hours chatting and drinking red wine. My dad always jokes that if Ben had spent as much time hunting fugitives as hunting me we'd have caught more!

Suddenly, people started approaching us as a pair – the Mr and Mrs Smith of *Hunted*! Ben was headhunted to take part in the US version of the series later that year and he invited me to go out there with him. I didn't need to be asked twice! By now I loved travel and would take any opportunity to see new places. In America, if you're on TV they think you're really famous. I wasn't, of course. Nevertheless, I got treated like a star and they asked me to come and visit the set where I met the deputy for the show, Theresa Payton, who had been the first female Chief Information Officer for the White House. The White House! Now that was really cool. Theresa and I got on well – we went for dinner, our kids became friendly, and when they all came to London we hosted them, taking them out for meals and around all the tourist sites.

'You know, Danni, it would be great if we all worked together,' she said one day. Theresa owned a cybersecurity company, a fantastic business made up of former White House staff. By then Ben had experience of digital surveillance and I had also entered the world of online investigations through a very odd route – football.

Hunted was now a regular series for Channel 4 and we shot two series a year for several years. Fortunately, most of my former Met colleagues were quite positive about the show, though some expressed surprise I would even entertain a TV career, despite it being a minor role. In between filming I had to find work to support myself and, since the world of investigations had already shifted from person to person infiltration to online, it felt natural to upgrade the skillset I already possessed. Ben taught open source intelligence, a form of online investigations. Someone on *Hunted* had a cyber company in Canada and suggested we take these courses and that's how we started to move into the online investigation world together. It felt very much like a natural progression. Then, the football stuff came along.

I was approached by the head of security for a Premier League team – a former police officer – to gather intelligence on what was going on outside the ground during game days, both online and physically, that could cause alarm or issues for the club, players and supporters, and I piggy-backed Ben into it. Then, we had a meeting with the club, where we identified a gap in their online security, demonstrating the vulnerabilities online, both for the club and individual players. It was easy enough to show that, if we had malicious intent, we could get their telephone numbers, passwords and hack into their accounts using entirely legal tools. This was 'open source' investigation: piecing bits of data together to complete a jigsaw. It freaked them out when we showed them a report on their digital footprint.

'The point is, if it is online and you are attached to it, we will find it,' I concluded. After the meeting we went for coffee in a local cafe.

'We can do this,' I said. I knew we could help clubs and players. Despite many of the welfare managers and physical security stating they had this 'online bodyguard work' under control, it was pretty clear they didn't. There were lots of other issues out there and we felt many of the other Premier League clubs could use our services too. We hadn't quite worked out the finer details, but I knew we could help them across multiple platforms. So we started working with football clubs.

One day, we got a call to come in to speak to a player at

another club. It was all a little mysterious. They wouldn't tell us much on the phone, but when we arrived at the meeting with the player and his agent we were told it was all very sensitive and everything was highly confidential. It appeared that our fella – who was in a serious, long-term relationship – had been away for pre-season training when he'd behaved a little stupidly with some girls he met. Now those girls – or people acting for them – were trying to blackmail him, but he didn't know who it was. All he had was an email address. He asked us to find out who was behind the operation.

We quickly established a good rapport. The fact we weren't middle-aged men in grey suits and could talk to the players on their level probably helped. Players had real life 'welfare managers' who took care of their day-to-day needs, but we were being asked to do the job for them online, like digital bodyguards. It was especially important for some of the players who, though talented footballers, weren't particularly blessed with smarts. This particular player was being evasive but I told him in no uncertain terms: 'Look, mate, I can't help you unless you're straight with me. I don't care who you slept with but if you don't tell me I can't help you.'

He rolled his eyes and then said: 'Okay, I have an incline of who it could be.'

I burst out laughing. *Incline!* Ben kicked me under the sofa, an instruction to stop laughing at our new client.

'If everyone else leaves I'll tell you,' he said. So after his agent left the room he blurted it all out, admitting all the things he got up to during his pre-season training. I reassured him that we could help him, and we did, securing him very good results. So good, in fact, that he came back to us several times with other friends who needed help.

This was how the idea for 'digital bodyguards' was born. We had been working with our football contacts and we hammered out the details with Theresa. She worked for a lot of high-net-worth individuals, and though most had extensive real-world security on their assets, few considered their online security. Since people – and especially celebrities – were getting hacked a lot we would offer to look after their security online. We developed the whole programme, acting both reactively and proactively, to ensure their safety and deter hackers. Ben and I work really well together. He is very career-focused and though he likes to say he's laid-back, he's a real grafter, just like me. While he's the more technical out of the two of us, I'm the problem-solver. I like putting the pieces of the puzzle together.

The business took off , and now we look after a lot of CEOs and CFOs, who are the main targets for online crime. It's funny – they'll always tell us they don't have anything out there, that they are invulnerable to attack, but we can always find the weaknesses. We pretend to be the bad guys and we probe for weak spots, entry points, and quite often find them in the family, the teenage kids whose Instagram accounts are wide open. Then, once we've completed our initial report, we'll carry on monitoring their security afterwards. We have our own company and we're exclusively employed by Theresa's company in a capacity as directors for Europe, Middle East and Africa.

Introducing Ben to the kids was quite straightforward.

They had seen him on TV first so they had an idea what he was like already. Fortunately, Albert was very young when he came into our lives so he didn't bat an eyelid, and Amelia adored him from the start. The fact that Amelia and Ben are both huge Manchester City fans helped, and they go to games a lot together, something they still do to this day. She has him wrapped around her little finger!

At first we spent time living in Alderley Edge, Cheshire, before moving to Ashford in Kent. But I always yearned to live abroad again. I had loved the lifestyle in France. It felt more accommodating to families, a gentler pace of life and I feared that our options were about to be diminished by Brexit. When we first got together I was always banging on about how I wanted to live overseas, but Ben was never sure – until Kent. That pushed him over the edge. He came to meet me off the train one day.

'Do you still want to live abroad?'

'Yes, why?

'Let's do it. Let's move to Spain. I want to go.'

It was so out of the blue.

'Why now? What changed your mind?'

'I've just heard these kids on the train speaking to their mum and the way they were talking to her, it was disgusting. It was like being in an episode of Jeremy Kyle. I don't want the kids to grow up like that. Let's go!'

'Let's do it.'

I booked the flights to Alicante on my phone and we came over to Spain in August 2019. We hired a car and drove along the coast until we came to a lovely town where both our families had visited when we were kids. There was something about the place that made us both feel instantly relaxed and at home.

'This is the place,' we agreed. 'We'll live here.'

We took the kids out of school, sold everything we owned on eBay and moved a month later with four suitcases, and we haven't looked back since. We received our residency cards a day before Brexit. I love it out here. The kids have spent the past four years in Spain so they are trilingual, Ben and I run our business from home and occasionally fly back to the UK for filming engagements, and are fortunate to enjoy a wonderful European lifestyle. I really couldn't ask for more.

Today, I couldn't be happier. I wake up every day and feel overwhelmed with gratitude at the thought that I get to do a brilliant job with a partner that I love and I can be there for my kids too.

Our work is mainly online, so we can base ourselves anywhere and now, if my child has an appointment or if they're sick, I don't have to worry about letting anyone down. I enjoyed an exciting career with the police force and I'm pleased I took the opportunities when they came along, but I have no regrets about leaving. It set me on a whole new path in the entertainment world and led me to Ben, so how bad can it be? I look at my daughter moving into a new phase in her life and I can see how mature and worldly she is at eighteen. We're the best of friends these days and, though I regret I couldn't be there for her more when she was little, I'm happy to have given her the chance to live in different countries and experience other cultures and languages. It's opened so many doors for her and will stand her in good stead throughout her life. As for my life – well, it's been a wild ride so far, I had to buy a lot of crack on the way, but it has all been worth it in the end. The question is – what comes next? I just can't wait to find out!

Epilogue

In 2019, I had gone back to work for the Met as a civilian. It was only for a short time while they tried to get on top of a mountain of old cases. They'd had a recruitment drive to bring in ex and retired cops on very attractive terms where we weren't required to do shifts and our pay was double that of serving officers. It was a simple case of too many crimes and not enough experience and officers to deal with them. And at that point in my life I was very happy to help out. In fact, I'd really enjoyed it. We were in Empress State Building in West Brompton, I worked the hours that suited me, and my best friend was in the same building, so we'd meet for lunch or after work for drinks. It was a really great few months, though I was shocked at the mess the Met were in. I'd been tasked with sifting through the cases in the Sexual Offences Unit in order to get on top of the caseload. There was a huge backlog of crimes and the officers who were assigned these cases simply weren't experienced enough. One girl on my unit had six months' service and she was being sent off to investigate rape allegations and serious sexual offences. She didn't know what she was doing. I felt bad for her. It wasn't her fault. Every officer in that unit had so many crimes on their books. They didn't know where to start. It was a case of going through them one by one and assessing if they could proceed or not. Slowly, methodically, we'd got through them until the files were in a much better state.

I'd enjoyed being back on a team again, reconnecting with old friends from Tower Hamlets and putting my skills and experience to good use. So when I got an email inviting me to take part in a new direct-entry scheme that would allow me to return as an inspector, my ears had pricked up. I wasn't so much interested in the rank, but the financial security was attractive. After five years of managing a freelance life, I yearned for a steady and reliable income stream and some routine. And over those last few months working in the Met, I'd felt valued and appreciated. So I'd considered re-joining the force. In fact, I took the fitness test, the medicals and the interview, and when I passed them all, the Met had made me a very attractive offer. The job had more flexibility, more money and more scope than I could have expected and I'd been sorely tempted to take it.

'You know I'll support you, whatever you choose,' Ben told me one night when we were talking it over. TV work was fun but it was intermittent and not a reliable source of income for either of us. By then we had been working with the football clubs for some time, helping to support players as their online welfare managers. We'd been wondering how we could pursue more investigative work online – and that was when the offer had come in to work with Theresa's company. I had faced a straight choice – returning to the Met or going into business with Ben and working for Theresa.

For a while I'd weighed up the relative merits of each. The police work had been great but I wondered whether it would be quite so enjoyable once I was obliged to do shifts and the civilian status no longer protected me from criticism. Besides, the opportunity with Theresa meant I could continue to work from home on my own hours.

'I don't think I can go back,' I had said to Ben. 'I think there is only forward for me, and for us. We have to take this opportunity to develop our skills and our company.'

It was the right decision and one that has allowed us to expand our area of expertise as well as move abroad in our pursuit of a balanced, happy lifestyle. Still, for a while, I had entertained the idea of returning to the police.

I have no regrets about my time on the force. On the contrary, I was proud to serve in one of Britain's vital emergency services. I realize that the Met has come in for a lot of criticism in the last few years, and rightly so. Despite employing a lot of good coppers it has fostered a culture of misogyny and the reports of racism have resulted in some shocking cases. And, as with any large, bureaucratic institution, a lot of time and resource seem to have been thrown into covering up rather than addressing the issues. It is no coincidence that I was one of the only women on my UC team and that I left the Met when I did. There are deep structural issues that appear to prevent women from joining and then progressing in their careers in the force, especially if they have families. There is very little support there for them, and yet, at the same time, it appears that some women are promoted despite not being qualified or the best person for the role – a box-ticking exercise for management – which is both detrimental and offensive. Attitudes form just one aspect of this problem, policies and programmes must also change in order to redress the balance. It is time to introduce a more compassionate framework for officers with families and make a career in policing an attractive long-term career option for all, especially for single parents.

I would hope those issues are now being looked at and addressed so that the police force is a viable employer, no matter what your age or stage in life. As it stands, I have no hesitation in recommending it as an excellent career choice for any young person. The police force gave me the confidence, opportunities and skills that made me who I am today. Not only that, but I also had amazing experiences working in borough and undercover. I loved working with the UC unit and still, to this day, our company works with the police to help develop their online investigations skills. Unfortunately, a lack of resources means that they are often reactive instead of proactive when it comes to online investigations, which is where so much crime takes place these days. They are hampered by outdated rules and bureaucracy – another area of policing ripe for overhaul!

The point is – you need to keep up with the way things are moving. Nowadays everything is online – if you go onto Craigslist and type in *Charles* or *Charlie* you can easily buy drugs that way. Where there is a demand, there is usually a supply somewhere. Dealers are becoming more sophisticated and ingenious. However, whether they are dealing in stairwells or on the internet, I don't see a huge benefit to prosecuting individuals for selling a few wraps of heroin. It's never going to stop them and besides, you're only picking off the foot soldiers. The bosses keep themselves at arm's length from the business and their hands clean. If you ask me, the police should be concentrating resources on tackling trafficking and sex crimes. That's where they could be making a real difference to people's lives. There are extremely serious abuses taking place that people don't even know about. On the dark web you can find things that may look quite innocent or inconspicuous but when you click on them you discover a site for sex trafficking or child abuse. It's more common than most people imagine and occasionally, in the course of investigations for our business, we have identified people at risk. In those cases, we have communicated our findings to the authorities.

Now that I have some slight public profile I get asked all the time: 'What's your opinion on regulating drugs?' And until quite recently I thought – *Well, it's illegal and anyone who does it should be punished.* But actually, my opinion has changed over the years and when I sat down and really thought about it I wondered how much positive change we had brought about in all those years catching dealers on the streets. For a long time I had put all my covert experiences to the back of my mind. That part of my life was over so I had closed the door to those memories. Now I examined them again and I recalled my sense of unease in giving evidence against the young lads dealing in small quantities of ecstasy or ketamine. I allowed myself to remember the time I had returned to Cumbria to give evidence against the young